A Taste of
Puerto Rico

Traditional and New Dishes from the Puerto Rican Community

A TASTE OF PUERTO RICO

Yvonne Ortiz

A DUTTON BOOK

DUTTON
Published by the Penguin Group
Penguin Books USA Inc., 375 Hudson Street,
New York, New York 10014, U.S.A.
Penguin Books Ltd, 27 Wrights Lane, London W8 5TZ, England
Penguin Books Australia Ltd, Ringwood, Victoria, Australia
Penguin Books Canada Ltd, 10 Alcorn Avenue,
Toronto, Ontario, Canada M4V 3B2
Penguin Books (N.Z.) Ltd, 182–190 Wairau Road,
Auckland 10, New Zealand

Penguin Books Ltd, Registered Offices:
Harmondsworth, Middlesex, England

First published by Dutton, an imprint of Dutton Signet, a division of Penguin Books USA Inc.
Distributed in Canada by McClelland & Stewart Inc.

First Printing, June, 1994
10 9 8 7 6 5 4 3 2

 REGISTERED TRADEMARK—MARCA REGISTRADA

LIBRARY OF CONGRESS CATALOGING-IN-PUBLICATION DATA

Ortiz, Yvonne.
    A taste of Puerto Rico : traditional and new dishes from the Puerto Rican community / Yvonne
Ortiz.
        p.   cm.
    ISBN 0-525-93812-5
    1. Cookery. Puerto Rican.   I. Title.
TX716.P8078   1994
641.597295—dc20   93-46165
                                                                                        CIP

Printed in the United States of America
Set in Palatino
Designed by Eve L. Kirch

*To my son, Alexito,
and all the Puerto Ricans on the U.S.A. mainland
who need to learn about our culinary traditions
from a distance.*

Acknowledgments

In 1989 this book seemed only a dream. Since then, many people have worked hard to make it a happy reality. I am grateful to you all. I would like to acknowledge:

My son for being patient and understanding. Madeline Morel, my agent, and Carole DeSanti and Julia Moskin, my editors; Sharon Pinsker, Ed Manchess, Eric Weinstein, and all the residents of Su Casa; John Haney, my proofreader, who also assisted in the recipe testing and development; Federica Bennett for turning a mess of notes into a manuscript; Dolores Gonzalez, my kitchen assistant; Yoly Sanchez and Milagros Marcano for research material; Dr. Maricel Precilla, my mentor; Fern Berman, Dalia Carmel, Elsa Ayala, and Angel Alvelo; Cara DeSilva at *New York Newsday;* my mother, father, and brother; and Mauricio Redondo.

Contents

Introduction

When I was growing up in Cayey, Puerto Rico, I could only sample the island's vast and diverse cuisines. Cayey is a small town located in the center of the island. It is surrounded by mountains and situated near the coastal town of Salinas. Its location gives the town a breezy warmth year-round that feels like spring on the mainland. During my childhood, the town consisted of only a few streets, a main plaza, and a church. There were only three restaurants, which served what would be considered "home cooking."

Even though the island is only a hundred miles long and thirty-five miles wide, there are marked regional differences in the names given to foods, their preparation, and the dishes themselves. It was when I entered the University of Puerto Rico in 1974 and went to live in a boardinghouse that my first real exposure to the diversity of our cuisine started.

Girls from all over the island attended the university. By becoming friends with many of them I was able to visit towns that otherwise would still be unknown to me except for the names on the map. Every town, or almost every one, is renowned for a special dish, fruit, or vegetable. For example, I tasted *mabí*, a fermented drink made from the bark of the *mabí* tree, which is somewhat like a cross between root beer and sarsaparilla, in Juana Díaz. Many people claim it is the best *mabí* in Puerto Rico. I also tried Villaalba's tomatoes; Ponce's *quenepas*, a fruit with a big pit and pink flesh; and Vieques's famous *bilí*, *quenepas* soaked in rum and marinated in the bottle for a few weeks. The rum is then strained and served.

When I was younger, I visited my maternal grandmother in Humacao every summer. As a curious teenager I wandered around the town looking for something interesting to do. One possibility was to eat lunch in the *fonda*, a kind of casual restaurant like the French *bistro* or Italian *trattoria*. The menu usually had typical peasant fare: tripe soup, boiled root vegetables, and rice and beans. These occasions became a ritual for me every summer, something I looked forward to all year.

Little did I know that some ten years later I would not only become a chef, but that I would also be an ambassador for our food. After completing my graduate studies, and feeling very sure of myself, I came to New York to pursue a dream: to study the culinary arts. I went through the entire spectrum, institutional as well as commercial cooking.

My training in classical French cuisine and its basic techniques allowed me to enter a new world. As a Puerto Rican I learned to cook for the American palate, but always with a tropical splash that was instinctive to me. One day I decided that it was time to go back to my ethnic and culinary roots. I was already fascinated with other countries' food histories. Why not investigate my people and how our food habits came to be what they are today?

For many years Puerto Ricans have been characterized as eating only rice and beans. Even though Puerto Ricans form the largest group of Hispanics living in cities like New York, little or nothing was known about the richness of our food culture. The traditional cuisine is the result of three heritages: the native, the Spanish, and the African. The cuisine is accentuated by features here and there from other groups who, even though they may have stayed for only a short time, left us

xii

some gastronomic presents. We even have some Italian and Chinese influences.

The growing number of second- and third-generation Puerto Ricans, including my son, on the mainland inspired me to write this book. Five centuries of culinary history have brought about significant changes in our eating habits. From the natives, with their mostly vegetarian diet, to the thousands of people in New York who celebrate the annual Puerto Rican Day Parade, we have a rainbow of flavors and traditions. With my most sincere intention of sharing all the valuable information that I have come across in recent years, this book was born. I hope it will give a better understanding of why we are the rainbow people and why our cuisine is diverse in colors and flavors.

Yvonne Ortiz
New York City
June 1994

A HISTORICAL AND CULINARY JOURNEY

Christopher Columbus discovered the island of Puerto Rico on his second voyage while looking for new lands to claim for the Spanish king and queen. When Spanish explorers (and later settlers) came to Puerto Rico, they found the Taíno people, members of the Arawak tribe, living there. The Arawaks were the dominant group in the Caribbean at that time; the Spanish called them "Indians," because Columbus was not at all correct in guessing where he was.

The Taínos had a structured society with a chief called a *cacique*. They grew food in gardens next to the *bohíos* (huts) in which they lived. The carefully tended gardens were known as *kunukus*. The main crops cultivated by the Taínos were *yuca* (cassava), corn, yams, and *yautía* (taro root). They also grew peanuts and a vegetable similar to the water chestnut called *lerén*. Fruits such as guava, soursop, pineapple, and sea grapes grew wild. Other foods that grew wild were black-eyed peas and lima beans.

Yuca was a staple food of the Taínos. The main food prepared with *yuca* was *casabe*, a flat bread that was eaten daily.

Yuca was an important staple because wheat did not grow well in the soil of the island and had to be imported from Spain. There were periods as long as eight years when a supply ship would not come! *Casabe* was often the only bread available; it was even used as the Host for Holy Communion. It is still eaten today. Taínos also used *yuca* to make vinegar, which was an important seasoning since they did not use salt in cooking. *Ajíes caballeros*, very hot peppers, were another popular seasoning.

Corn was a major food in the Taíno diet. Foods to be cooked on an open fire were wrapped in corn husks, later replaced by plantain leaves brought to the island by African slaves, but the grain was very important to the island diet and culture.

Taínos used very little domestic equipment in food preparation. The two main cooking utensils, the *olla* (pot) and the *burén* (flat griddle put directly on the fire), used for toasting, panbroiling, and making *casabe*, were made of clay. Taínos cooked their food over a *fogón*, a hearth of three stones, with a fire made from leaves and sticks. The natives' diet was mainly vegetarian. They did, however, eat some meat, such as iguana, and they hunted and fished for shellfish, tortoise, seabirds, and other game.

Foods introduced by the Spanish include chick-peas, cilantro, eggplant, onions, and garlic. Many foods native to Mexico and South America came to the island during the European explorations of the seventeenth and eighteenth centuries. Potatoes came from the Andes, passion fruit from Brazil, chayote, papaya, avocado, and cocoa from Mexico. Breadfruit was brought from Tahiti to feed the African slaves in the eighteenth century and remained a staple when slavery was abolished in the nineteenth century. The coconut palm tree was introduced by the Spanish, but fruits like pears, peaches, and apples did not adapt well to the growing conditions on the island. Two other foods, essential to the Spanish daily diet, that did not thrive at all in the island's soil were olives and grapes. Without olive oil, lard became the cooking fat of choice.

Coffee came in 1736, and along with sugarcane was the

backbone of the island's economy through the first half of this century. Rum, introduced to the island by the Spanish, has become the favorite liquor over the years. Today Puerto Rico is the biggest producer of rum in the world.

The African slave trade brought important foods and techniques to the island's cuisine. The most significant of the former were green pigeon peas, plantain, yams, and okra. The African population also developed many coconut dishes, which are still quite popular. Their favorite technique was frying, which quickly became our most popular way of cooking.

Other groups that visited the island and left culinary presents were the Dutch (Edam cheese), the Italians (macaroni and chicken), and the Chinese (dumplings). The Chinese came to the area after slavery had been abolished. They worked in the sugar and coffee fields. By the end of the nineteenth century all these elements had shaped what we consider our national cuisine. By 1848 the first restaurant, La Mallorquina, was established in Old San Juan. *El Cocinero Puertorriqueño*, the island's first cookbook, was published in 1849.

In a traditional Puerto Rican diet, a typical breakfast consists of *café con leche* (coffee with hot milk) and a piece of bread with butter. Today the morning meal is more American style: bacon, eggs, home fries, and pancakes. Once, lunch would have been boiled root vegetables and codfish. To these have now been added fast-food items such as pizza, burgers, sandwiches, and the very popular salads sold in salad bars. Dinner almost always consists of rice, beans, and a meat dish, preceded by a soup. Other choices include *tostones* (fried green plantains), fried yellow plantains, and *yuca con mojo* (cassava in garlic sauce).

Traditionally, Puerto Rican cuisine did not include much in the way of vegetables. A typical green salad would consist of lettuce, tomatoes, cucumbers, and canned peas and corn. Other vegetables eaten were *chayote* and eggplant. They were usually part of a stewed dish.

Nouvelle Cuisine brought a new spectrum of foods to the island. From breakfast to dessert, different choices are now available. Fresh pasta, salmon, lamb, and a better variety of vegetables can now be purchased. Today at the typical restaurant you can get dishes like shrimp in creole sauce, served with broccoli or cauliflower. Typical desserts such as *flan* (egg custard), *tembleque* (coconut custard), and guava with white cheese have been replaced by lighter and more sophisticated preparations. Mango jelly roll, passion fruit cheesecake, and fresh fruit salad with kiwi are part of the present repertoire.

Holidays and festive occasions have a special menu: roast suckling pig, rice with green pigeon peas, and goat or veal stew. This menu is still followed even on the mainland. American holidays like Thanksgiving and Easter have become part of our traditional celebrations, but we give them a very Puerto Rican touch. Turkey is seasoned with *adobo*, the stuffing is made with beef *picadillo*, and roast pork is eaten on Easter Sunday.

Although we are not big on dairy products, we do produce a white cheese called *queso de hoja*. On the island it is sold fresh; here on the mainland we can get it packaged. Among the typical food establishments are the *fonda* (diner-type restaurant) and the *plaza de mercado* (indoor farmers' market that usually includes stands to buy prepared food).

The last element in our cuisine is American. When we became part of the United States in 1898, American foods and eating habits were combined with traditional ones. After the Depression we suffered the effects of the Second World War and a massive migration to the United States.

By 1950 things were changing on the island. The electric blender replaced the *pilón* (mortar and pestle) in making important basics such as *recaíto*, as women started to enter the work force. At the same time, tourism became an important factor in the island's economy. With the boom, our cuisine had to be adapted to suit the palates of our visitors. It was also a time when the first significant cookbooks written by Puerto Rican women were published. On the mainland, Puerto Ricans struggled to get used to the new environment. La Marketa was established in New York in 1936. This market, located under the train tracks of Metro North in East Harlem, became a way of preserving the diet and the culinary traditions of the Caribbean. It was and is a primary meeting place, routinely drawing shoppers from all over the city. Until recently, ingredients such as cilantro, sweet chili peppers, and *mabí* could be found only in La Marketa.

The *bodegas,* small grocery stores, became a symbol of our cultural identity. These stores, started by Spanish immigrants at the end of the nineteenth century, were located at the heart of prominent Puerto Rican neighborhoods like the Lower East Side and South Brooklyn. The best thing about *bodegas* is that they make Puerto Rican ingredients widely available.

Puerto Rican New Cuisine showed up around 1978, an offshoot of Nouvelle Cuisine, which started in France, then spread to the United States, and soon reached the island. This movement brought about a considerable refinement of our traditional peasant dishes. There were innovative combinations of ingredients and more elegant presentations. Fruits found their way into classical sauces; recipes were lighter. There were fewer fried foods; lard was almost completely eliminated. Balsamic vinegar and kiwi fruit were introduced. People started to become more educated about the dining experience. Magazines such as *Bon Appétit* and *Cuisine* became available in San Juan. It was just the beginning of a new era for our gastronomy. Puerto Rican New Cuisine, although not yet well known outside the island, started to redefine our food culture. Chefs like Giovanna Huyke and Alfredo Ayala are considered the pioneers of the movement.

In the 1980s our diet was redefined, especially by health issues that slowly started to make an impression in the last ten years. Lard, used for centuries, was replaced by corn and olive oils. (Traditionally, olive oil was used only for salads and pickling.) Low-cholesterol cooking and foods gradually became part of the daily diet. Our famous fritters are now made with annatto oil instead of lard!

Back on the mainland at about the same time, the *casita* concept was born. It is truly a phenomenon of our culture. *Casitas* are little houses that resemble the traditional *bohíos,* the huts that date back to Taíno times. They are built in gardens throughout New York and are used for community activities like after-school programs, voter-registration drives, and big day-long picnics. Food, of course, plays an important and essential role in the *casitas*. Traditions are strengthened through special activities such as the celebration of Three Kings Day (Epiphany) and the Puerto Rican Day Parade, as well as daily activities.

The 1990s brought back to the island's cuisine the *fonda*, or traditional family-style restaurant. Casita Blanca, the best-known *fonda* in San Juan, has become a showcase for our rediscovered traditional foods.

Puerto Ricans travel constantly between the island and the mainland. A melding of new and traditional cooking in many homes as well as in food establishments has resulted. I hope to reflect this trend in *A Taste of Puerto Rico.*

THE BASICS: THE PUERTO RICAN PANTRY
(La Despensa Puertorriqueña)

Like every cuisine, Puerto Rican cooking has some staple ingredients. These are a result of five hundred years of culinary exchanges. Although some ingredients have been replaced because of health concerns and lifestyle changes, the basic staples are fairly consistent with those of our ancestors.

Some ingredients may not be immediately familiar to you, although most of them are readily available. I have included a mail-order guide to help those who live in areas where the ingredients might not be easy to obtain.

The ingredients used in traditional Puerto Rican cooking, like the dishes that showcase them, are a result of a wonderfully tangled heritage. These are everyday grocery items for people on the island as well as here in the United States. Sweet chili peppers, passion fruit, and papayas add color and fragrance to produce counters throughout the country. Varieties of these foods grown in the United States make them easier to find and more affordable.

Besides finding typical foods when you shop for Puerto Rican pantry items, you will find a reflection of our culture and cuisine. You will have the opportunity to see, touch, and smell the ingredients that make our dishes unique.

Aceite de maíz (corn oil) has replaced lard as the cooking fat of choice. It is used for frying, cooking rice, stewing, and braising.

Adobo is a basic dry seasoning mix made of salt, black pepper, garlic, and onion powder. It is used for meats, poultry, pork, and seafood. *Adobo* can be purchased bottled, with or without black pepper. (See recipe, page 15.)

Alcaparrado, a bottled mixture of olives, capers, and diced pimiento imported from Spain, is used mainly in bean stews, pickled fish, and braised meat dishes.

Annatto or *achiote* seeds have been used for centuries. Annatto replaced hard-to-find saffron in colonial cooking. The seeds can be ground and sprinkled or mixed into soups, pastry dough, or stews. Annatto does not have the delicate flavor of saffron but imparts a bright yellow color that can turn an everyday dish into a festive presentation. To make annatto oil, heat two cups of olive oil in a small saucepan. Add ½ cup annatto seeds (available at all *bodegas* and many supermarkets) and cook about 5 minutes over low heat. When the oil is a rich orange color, remove, let cool, and strain.

Bacalao is dry salted codfish. It is always soaked in water and cooked before being incorporated into recipes. It is usually sold whole, with some bones and skin, or as a fillet, skinless and with few or no bones. The two main preparations in which *bacalao* is used are salads and stews.

To cook *bacalao*, first soak it in water to cover overnight. Then put it in a pot with cold water to cover, and bring to a boil. When the water boils, pour it off and repeat with fresh cold water. Repeat once more, then taste the *bacalao*. If it still seems excessively salty, repeat one more time, then cool and shred.

Calabaza is West Indian pumpkin, a vegetable with green skin and bright, firm yellow flesh. It is used mainly in stews. It can also be used to make fritters, soups, and custards. *Calabaza* is available year-round and is sold whole or cut in pieces.

The whole squash can be round or pear-shaped. It can be somewhat difficult to determine if it is ripe and ready to use. Look for a squash with a dull rind and a solid stem attached. It should be heavy for its size. If you are buying just a piece, look for bright yellow flesh. A whole squash can be stored at room temperature for up to a month. Cut it into pieces, remove all of the seeds, wrap it tightly in plastic wrap, and refrigerate. Pieces can be stored this way for up to a week. It can also be frozen. If *calabaza* is not available, you can substitute acorn squash.

Cilantro (coriander), is also known as *cilantrillo* or *culantrillo*. It is an herb with green leaves that looks somewhat like parsley. Cilantro is available year-round almost everywhere. Make sure the roots are still attached. To store, wrap in moist paper towel and place in the refrigerator. Wash well and let sit in cold water just before use.

Coco is coconut. That used for cooking purposes is in the mature stage and has a hairy brown surface. It is also known as *coco seco* (dry coconut). Coconut milk is the liquid extracted from the coconut meat. Coconut cream, a very sweet canned coconut product, is used mostly in the preparation of drinks like the *piña colada*. Both are available in supermarkets.

Gandules (green pigeon peas) are our national bean. They are used to prepare our famous dish, *arroz con gandules*— yellow rice with green pigeon peas (see recipe, page 171.) These peas, of African origin, are sold on the island fresh, canned, or frozen. On the mainland you will most likely find them frozen or canned. They are also sold dried.

Guanábana, soursop, a fruit with green skin and white, sweet pulp, was traditionally used to make drinks, including the popular *champola*. Fresh soursops are hard to find on the mainland, but frozen pulp and concentrate are available year-round.

Habichuelas (beans) are part of the real basic Puerto Rican cuisine. The most popular beans on the island are the *rosada* (pink), *blanca* (white), *marca diablo* (red kidney), and *garbanzo* (chick-pea). In traditional cooking, dried beans were soaked overnight, cooked, and incorporated into the recipe. (See recipe for cooking dried beans, page 172.) Canned beans can also be used.

Jamón de cocinar is a cured (smoked) ham usually sold in thick slices. It is an essential ingredient in the traditional *sofrito*. It is also used as a flavor enhancer in stews, yellow-rice dishes, and braised meats such as Puerto Rican pot roast (*carne mechada*). (See recipe, page 148.) If smoked ham is not available, you can use ham steak or any other lightly smoked ham.

Lechosa, papaya, grown on the island is very different from the type we are used to seeing here on the mainland. When mature, the skin color is a much brighter color (almost golden) than the Hawaiian fruit that is so common in the United States. The flesh is thick, with an almost coral-red color. Another big difference is the size. Puerto Rican papayas can reach 20 inches in length and weigh as much as 10 pounds. We eat papaya fresh as is or in milkshakes. Green papaya is cooked with sugar and spices. It is a traditional dessert served with white cheese. This variety of papaya is also grown in Florida, Mexico, and the Philippines. Hispanic markets carry it mostly during the summer months. Hawaiian papaya, available almost year-round, can be substituted. Look for a fruit that is almost yellow. If it is only partly ripe, leave it at room temperature for a few more days. Refrigerate only when the fruit is completely ripe.

Parcha, passion fruit, is an oval-shaped fruit, native to Brazil. The variety grown on the island has a light yellow color. The ones we get here come mostly from New Zealand and are purple. Both types have a hard shell with seeds surrounded by fleshy deep-orange pulp. For many years passion fruit was used mainly to prepare a delicious thirst-quenching juice, *refresco de parcha.* As the New Cuisine became popular on the island, this "liquid gold" found its way into ice creams, sorbets, and innovative sauces. The fresh fruit can be expensive, but today passion fruit concentrate is available almost everywhere. It is sold frozen or in liquid form.

If you are lucky enough to find fresh passion fruit, look for ones that are large and heavy. They are usually sold by the piece. The fruit will be ripe when the skin is wrinkled. It can be kept at room temperature for a few days until you are ready to use it. It will also keep for about a week in the refrigerator. You can freeze the whole fruit in a plastic bag. When ready to use, simply cut in half and defrost the pulp.

Pimientos de cocinar, Italian frying peppers, are peppers with a thin skin and a mild flavor. They are usually from 3 to 5 inches long and about 2 inches wide. Their color varies from light green to bright red. Italian frying peppers are available fresh year-round. Look for shiny skin with no wrinkles. Store them in the refrigerator.

Plátano, plantain, is a relative of the banana. It is eaten green or ripe. Green plantain, or *plátano verde,* is the plantain at the unripened stage. It has a thick green skin and firm cream-colored flesh with a starchy taste. Store green plantains at room temperature; they will ripen slowly. If you refrigerate green plantains they will not ripen. Green plantain is used to make *mofongo, tostones,* and *pasteles.* (See Glossary.) *Plátano maduro* or *amarillo,* the yellow plantain at the ripe stage, has a sweet taste. When the plantain is greenish yellow it is called *pintón.* This means that it has black spots throughout the yellow skin. When the plantain is fully ripe it is also called *maduro.* Most dishes are made with the plantain at this stage, when the flesh is still firm. When the plantain turns completely black, it is made into a dessert called *dulce de plátano.* Ripe yellow plantains can be fried, baked, or boiled. They are also used in dishes like yellow plantain and meat pie. (See recipe, page 94.)

Recaíto is a raw mixture of Old and New World ingredients: *Recao* (green spiny leaf), *ajíes dulces* (sweet chili peppers), and *pimientos de cocinar* (Italian frying peppers) are native to the Caribbean. Garlic, onions, and cilantro came from Europe. Combined with tomato sauce, *alcaparrado,* and ham or fatback, and cooked slightly, *recaíto* becomes *sofrito.*

Salchichas, Vienna sausages, are a popular combination of beef, pork, and chicken sausage in a broth. They are only available canned.

Salsa de tomate, canned tomato sauce "Spanish style," is used in all stewed and braised dishes.

Sofrito consists of *recaíto* mixed with cooking ham or fatback, *alcaparrado,* and tomato sauce. This mixture is traditionally lightly sautéed in lard. Today lard has been replaced by corn or olive oil, and the fatback and ham have been largely eliminated. The Spanish settlers brought the *sofrito* (slightly cooked) concept to the island and adapted it to the new ingredients they found there.

Tamarindo, tamarind, is a pod-shaped fruit with brown skin. Large pits hold the pulp, which tends to be somewhat sour. It is eaten as a fruit, added to drinks, and mixed with sugar to make a compote. Store tamarind at room temperature or in the refrigerator.

Tocino, dry salt-cured pork (fatback), is a major ingredient of the traditional *sofrito* and yellow-rice dishes. White rice is also cooked with *tocino.* The fatback is diced and sautéed over medium heat. The fat rendered is then used to prepare other dishes. The golden brown, crispy pieces can be removed or incorporated into the dish.

Fatback is no longer used as often as it was in the past. Cholesterol-conscious cooks now opt for healthier versions of *sofrito* made with corn or olive oil. Store fatback wrapped in plastic in the refrigerator.

Viandas is the collective name for the many root vegetables and tubers that have been an important feature of Puerto Rican cooking since the time of the Taínos. Included in this category are *yautía, yuca, chayote, calabaza, apio, batata,* and *ñame.* All are starchy vegetables that should be bought when firm, and can be kept indefinitely in a cool place if left whole. They are used in *sancocho* and many other stews and soups. American pumpkin, potatoes, and sweet potatoes are acceptable substitutes, but you will sacrifice some flavor.

Vinagre generally means cider vinegar and is used mainly to marinate cubed steak and salad dressings. White vinegar is used to prepare *escabeche* dishes. Today balsamic and raspberry vinegars are used in dishes like pickled green bananas. (See recipe, page 37.)

3

SAUCES, DRESSINGS, SEASONINGS, AND MARINADES
(Salsas, Aderezos, y Marinadas)

The basic sauces in traditional Puerto Rican cooking are those based on *sofrito, escabeche, ajilimójili, mojito de ajo,* and *mojito isleño.* Our main sauce is a *sofrito* base that is used in stewing and braising.

Escabeche, a combination of olive oil, white vinegar, and spices, is used mainly for marinating. It is essential in seafood dishes eaten during Lent, such as *pescado en escabeche.*

Ajilimójili, a combination of sweet chili peppers, lemon, and garlic, is a sauce that can be improvised with freshly picked ingredients.

Mojito de ajo is a basic dipping sauce made with fresh garlic and olive oil. *Mojito de ajo* and *ajilimójili* do not require any cooking.

Mojito isleño is our best-known sauce. A combination of onions, olives, and tomato sauce, it is served with fritters and fried fish.

Other sauces have become part of our repertoire as part of the new Puerto Rican cuisine. Fruits have been incorporated into sauces like barbecue, Hollandaise, or vinaigrette, and Italian pesto has been adapted using cilantro instead of basil.

Adobo

Adobo is a basic seasoning in Puerto Rican cooking. It can be used for meats, poultry, pork, or seafood.

1 **tablespoon garlic powder**
1 **tablespoon onion powder**
1 **tablespoon dried oregano**
½ **tablespoon salt**
½ **tablespoon black pepper**

Mix all of the ingredients in a food processor or shake well in a glass jar.

Makes 4 tablespoons

Basic Recaíto
(Recaíto Básico)

This is the base for sofrito. *It can be made in large batches and frozen.*

- ½ medium yellow onion, diced
- 1 Italian frying pepper, seeded and diced
- 2 garlic cloves, peeled
- 3 sweet chili peppers, seeded
- 3 *recao* leaves (if *recao* leaves are unavailable, triple the amount of cilantro)
- 1 sprig cilantro

Combine all of the ingredients in a blender or food processor.

Makes ½ cup

NOTE: If using a blender, add some water or oil to the machine before mixing the ingredients.

Escabeche Sauce
(Salsa de Escabeche)

When Cara DeSilva, New York Newsday food writer, interviewed me about Puerto Rican cuisine for the first time, she was fascinated with the many dishes we make escabeche style.

Escabeche sauce is common throughout the island. White vinegar is used in traditional versions. New variations are being made with balsamic, red wine, and raspberry vinegars.

  1 cup olive oil
  3 medium yellow onions, sliced
  ½ cup white vinegar
  ½ tablespoon salt
  1 tablespoon black peppercorns
  4 bay leaves
  5 garlic cloves, peeled and chopped
  1 cup *alcaparrado*, drained and rinsed

Heat the oil in a nonreactive pan. Add the onion and sauté for 5 minutes. Reduce the heat. Add the remaining ingredients and cook over medium heat for 10 minutes.

Makes 3½ cups

NOTE: This sauce can be used with fried fish, poached chicken, or boiled *viandas* (root vegetables).

Sofrito Dipping Sauce
(Salsa de Sofrito)

A habit-forming sauce! Serve it with fish sticks or chicken cracklings.

- **1 tablespoon corn oil**
- **2 tablespoons Basic *Recaíto* (see page 16)**
- **1 tablespoon tomato paste**
- **1 tablespoon ketchup**

Heat the oil. Add the remaining ingredients and sauté lightly over medium heat for 3 minutes.

Makes ⅓ cup

Ajilimójili Sauce
(Salsa de Ajilimójili)

This traditional sauce is usually served with meats and fried fish. It is also good with tostones *(fried green plantain) or simply boiled* viandas *(root vegetables).*

3 garlic cloves, peeled
10 sweet chili peppers, seeded
1 teaspoon salt
1 teaspoon black pepper
   Juice of 3 lemons
½ cup olive oil

Grind all the dry ingredients in a mortar. Add the lemon juice and oil and mix well.

Makes 1 cup

NOTE: This sauce can also be prepared in a blender or food processor.

Traditional Garlic Dipping Sauce
(Mojito de Ajo Tradicional)

This is the classic sauce served over tostones *(fried green plantains). It can also be used for* viandas *(root vegetables). Watch out, it's habit forming!*

6 garlic cloves, peeled
1 cup olive oil
1 teaspoon salt

Crush the garlic cloves in a mortar. Add the oil and salt. Store, tightly covered, in the refrigerator.

Makes 1 cup

NOTE: This sauce can also be made in a blender or food processor.

Mojito Isleño

This traditional sauce comes from Salinas, a town on the southern coast of Puerto Rico. Almost everyone has a recipe for it. My version was inspired by the members of Villa Puerto Rico, one of the casitas *(see page 5). Many of them come from this beautiful part of the island.* Mojito Isleño *can be served with any of our classic fritters, such as* bacalaítos *(salt-cod fritters),* almojábanas *(rice-flour fritters) or* sorullitos *(cornmeal sticks).*

⅓ cup corn oil
1 medium yellow onion, chopped
1 cup tomato sauce
⅓ cup *alcaparrado,* drained, or manzanilla olives
2 bay leaves
2 Italian frying peppers, seeded and chopped
1 teaspoon salt
2 teaspoons black pepper
2 roasted red peppers, drained and cut into strips

Heat the oil in a heavy pot. Add the onion and sauté over medium heat until translucent. Add the rest of the ingredients and bring to a boil. Reduce the heat to low and cook for 15 minutes.

Makes 2⅓ cups

NOTE: You can use green bell peppers instead of the frying peppers and red onions instead of yellow, if desired.

Guava Barbecue Sauce
(Salsa de Guayaba para La Barbacoa)

Guavas grow wild on the island. Here they are rather expensive and sometimes hard to find. Frozen guava pulp works just fine in this delicious sauce. Brush this over ribs or chicken.

1 **cup frozen guava pulp, thawed**
1 **cup ketchup**
1 **tablespoon Dijon mustard**
2 **tablespoons sherry**

Thoroughly combine all of the ingredients.

Makes 2 cups

Guava Hollandaise Sauce
(Salsa Holandesa de Guayaba)

Here is a variation of the classic French sauce. It works well with poached lobster or shrimp and is also good over grilled fish, chicken, or beef. When I first made this sauce I asked my son, Alex, to help me peel the shrimp that would accompany it. He agreed because he couldn't resist the fragrant smell of guava!

3 **egg yolks**
1 **tablespoon fresh lemon juice**
3 **tablespoons frozen guava pulp, thawed (found in the juice section of the supermarket)**
¼ **pound (1 stick) unsalted butter**
½ **teaspoon salt**
½ **teaspoon white pepper**

Blend the egg yolks with the lemon juice and guava concentrate in a food processor or blender for about 10 seconds. Melt the butter over medium-low heat until it starts to bubble. While the butter is still bubbling, pour it slowly through the feed tube of the processor or into the running blender, until the sauce thickens. Season with salt and pepper.

Makes 1 cup

Guava Butter
(Mantequilla de Guayaba)

Guava preserves combined with butter and golden rum make a delicious spread for breakfast toast.

- ½ cup (1 stick) butter
- 3 tablespoons guava preserves
- ½ tablespoon golden rum

Combine all of the ingredients in a food processor.

Makes ¾ cup

Mango Vinaigrette
(Vinagreta de Mango)

When I was working for A Sense of Taste caterers, Cheryl Kleinman introduced me to sauces made with fresh mango.

Every time I go back home to Puerto Rico, I can't think of enough uses for the mangoes in my mother's backyard. This dressing is good with a simple salad of arugula, carrots, and celery.

1   cup mango purée (2 medium mangoes puréed in food
      processor)
⅓   cup cider vinegar
⅔   cup sunflower oil
3   tablespoons honey
1   teaspoon salt
1   teaspoon white pepper
2   tablespoons chopped fresh scallion for garnish

Combine all of the ingredients, except the scallion, in a blender or food processor. Transfer the mixture to a bowl and garnish with the scallion.

Makes 1¾ cups

Mango Mojito
(Mojito de Mango)

Mangoes came to the island via Brazil. The best ones are from Mayaguez, a town on the west coast. Mangoes and ginger are combined here to create a delicious condiment. Serve it with grilled fish or chicken.

- 1 **tablespoon brown sugar**
  Juice of 2 limes
- 1 **tablespoon chopped fresh ginger**
- 1 **scallion, chopped**
- ¼ **cup roughly chopped cilantro**
- 2 **medium mangoes, peeled and diced**
  Pinch salt

Thoroughly combine all of the ingredients.

Makes 1½ cups

Papaya and Tarragon Sauce
(Salsa de Papaya y Estragón)

Tarragon's delicate flavor combines perfectly with papaya. This sauce, with its subtle yellow color, offers an interesting alternative to our everyday red sauces and is very good with grilled fish or roasted chicken.

      2 **medium papayas, peeled and diced**
   1¼ **cups heavy cream**
     ¼ **cup dry sherry**
      2 **tablespoons fresh tarragon or 2 teaspoons dried**
          tarragon leaves
      1 **teaspoon salt**
      1 **teaspoon white pepper**

Purée the papaya and press through a sieve; set aside. In a saucepan over medium heat, reduce the heavy cream by about half. Add the remaining ingredients. Turn the heat to low and cook for 5 minutes. Cool the sauce to room temperature. Strain before serving.

Makes 2 cups

Cilantro Pesto
(Pesto de Cilantro)

This variation of the classic Italian sauce can be spread on grilled chicken or fish. For an interesting salad, combine it with cooked chayote and plum tomatoes.

- 2 cups cilantro
- ½ cup grated Parmesan cheese
- ⅓ cup chopped walnuts
- ¾ cup olive oil
- 4 garlic cloves, peeled
- 1 teaspoon black pepper
  Juice of 2 lemons

Thoroughly combine all of the ingredients in a food processor or blender.

Makes 1¼ cups

Cilantro Aïoli
(Aïoli de Cilantro)

This sauce is where the Mediterranean meets the Caribbean!

6 egg yolks
1 teaspoon Dijon mustard
   Salt and black pepper to taste
1 tablespoon fresh lemon juice
3 garlic cloves, peeled and crushed
1 cup loosely packed cilantro
1 cup light olive oil combined with 1 cup regular olive oil
1 tablespoon hot water

Place the egg yolks, mustard, salt, pepper, lemon juice, garlic, and cilantro in a blender or food processor. Process until the leaves are finely chopped. With the processor still running, slowly add the oil. The mixture should have the consistency of mayonnaise. Add the hot water, blend, and transfer to a glass container. Cover and refrigerate until ready to use.

Makes 2½ cups

Green Sauce
(Salsa Verde)

Nydia Velazquez, the first Puerto Rican woman to be elected to the U.S. Congress, likes to prepare mixed seafood cooked in salsa verde. You can also serve it over grilled fish, shrimp, or steamed lobster.

- ½ cup cilantro
- 5 garlic cloves
- 1 teaspoon salt
- 1⅓ cups olive oil
- ⅓ cup fresh lemon juice
- ½ teaspoon salt
- 2 teaspoons capers for garnish

Combine all of the ingredients except the capers in a food processor. Garnish with the capers.

Makes 1¾ cups

Butter-Rum Seafood Sauce
(Salsa de Mantequilla y Ron para Mariscos)

A simple sauce that enhances the flavor of poached seafood.

1½ **cups fish stock**
 1 **tablespoon golden rum (or to taste)**
 1 **tablespoon all-purpose flour combined with 1
     tablespoon melted butter**
 1 **teaspoon salt**
 1 **teaspoon black pepper**
    Chopped parsley for garnish

Bring the stock and rum to a boil. Turn the heat to low and whisk in the flour-butter mixture, a little at a time, until the sauce thickens. Turn the heat to medium-low and cook for 5 minutes, stirring constantly. Add the salt and pepper. Add parsley for garnish.

Makes 1½ cups

APPETIZERS AND FRITTERS
(Aperitivos y Frituras)

Fritters are everyday food in Puerto Rico. They are sold at fritter stands and incorporated into the daily menus in most homes. They are also served as appetizers.

Meat turnovers, or *empanadas*, fritters common to all Latin cuisines, are often eaten for breakfast. Seafood *empanadas* are usually eaten for lunch. Guava turnovers (made with puff pastry) are served for dessert, sprinkled with confectioners' sugar. Our most famous fritters, *tostones* (fried green plantains), are a traditional side dish. They are served with rice and beans, onion steak, or fried pork chops.

The Puerto Rican New Cuisine has turned this peasant fritter into a gourmet presentation by adding items like caviar and fancy seafoods. Other traditional appetizers are chicken nuggets and pickled green bananas. The latter are now combined with new ingredients like flavored vinegars to create interesting variations that can be found in elegant restaurants and on caterers' menus in the United States.

Note that unripe (green) bananas and plantains are *not* the same! See "The Basics" (page 11) for information.

Stuffed Papaya
(Papaya Rellena)

A light and refreshing brunch dish!

Boston lettuce
6 **small papayas, peeled, halved lengthwise, and seeded**
6 **tablespoons cottage cheese combined with 3**
   tablespoons mango, banana, kiwi, or strawberries,
   diced
Ground nutmeg for garnish

Arrange the lettuce on a platter. Put the papaya halves on top and stuff with the cottage-cheese mixture. Sprinkle with nutmeg to taste.

Serves 6

Puerto Rican White Cheese Marinated in Fresh Herbs

(Queso Blanco Puertorriqueño Marinado en Hierbas Frescas)

In this variation of fresh mozzarella cheese marinated in fresh herbs, the cilantro gives just the right tropical touch.

- 1½ **pounds Puerto Rican white cheese**
- 3 **cups olive oil**
- 4 **tablespoons coarsely chopped fresh basil**
- 4 **tablespoons coarsely chopped fresh cilantro**
- 2 **tablespoons coarsely chopped fresh thyme**
  Pinch black pepper

Set the cheese in a bowl. In another bowl, combine the oil, herbs, and pepper, then pour the mixture over the cheese. Marinate in the refrigerator overnight. Drain the cheese and slice.

Serves 6

Puerto Rican White Cheese and Tomato Salad

(Ensalada de Tomate y Queso Blanco Puertorriqueño)

Classical tomato salad with a Puerto Rican touch, served with cilantro pesto.

     2 **7-ounce packages Puerto Rican white cheese, sliced**
3 or 4 **medium tomatoes, sliced**
    ¼ **cup Cilantro Pesto (see page 28)**

Arrange the cheese and tomato slices on a platter. Pour the cilantro pesto over them. Refrigerate, covered, for at least 1 hour before serving.

Serves 6

Traditional Pickled Green Bananas
(Guineos Verdes en Escabeche)

This dish is a holiday staple on the island. You can prepare it with almost any root vegetable. You can use the basic Escabeche Sauce (see page 17) or the following combination.

    4 pounds unripe (green) bananas, unpeeled, cooked for
         20 minutes in 2 cups of milk plus 2 quarts of water
    ⅔ cup white vinegar
  1⅔ cups olive oil
    1 tablespoon salt
    ½ tablespoon black pepper
    1 cup *alcaparrado*
    4 bay leaves

Peel the bananas and cut them into ½-inch-thick slices. Combine the remaining ingredients in a nonreactive bowl. Add the bananas and toss well. Marinate for at least 1 hour before serving. Even better, marinate overnight.

Serves 6

NOTE: A variation of this traditional dish is made with balsamic vinegar and black Kalamata olives. See the following recipe.

Green Bananas in Balsamic Vinaigrette
(Guineos Verdes con Vinagre Balsámico)

*Faintly resembling potato salad, this dish makes an intriguing trop-
ical side dish for grilled chicken, fish, or beef. Sweet balsamic vinegar
from Italy and Kalamata olives from Greece add a cross-cultural di-
mension to this version of the classic* escabeche, *pickled green bananas.*

2 cups milk
2 quarts water
1 tablespoon salt
4 pounds unpeeled unripe (green) bananas, halved
   crosswise (do not peel)
⅔ cup balsamic vinegar
½ tablespoon black pepper
1⅔ cups light olive oil
1 cup Kalamata olives, pitted and sliced
4 bay leaves

In a soup kettle or large pot, bring the milk and water to a
boil. Add the salt and bananas. Bring to a boil again, then reduce the heat, and simmer until the bananas are cooked but
firm, 20 to 25 minutes.

Drain and peel the bananas, and cut them into ½-inch-thick
slices. In a large nonreactive bowl, mix the vinegar with the
black pepper. Whisk in the oil. Add the olives, bay leaves, and
bananas and toss well. Let stand at room temperature for at
least 1 hour before serving. This dish can be refrigerated overnight.

Serves 6

Traditional Tostones
(Tostones Tradicionales)

Traditionally, tostones *were eaten as a side dish with* bistec encebollado *(onion steak), a dish as standard as American meat and potatoes.* Tostones *can also be considered our French fries. Twice fried,* tostones *are crispy on the outside and meaty inside. They recently have become star appetizers in the new culinary repertoire of the island.*

2 **cups corn oil**
3 **green plantains, peeled and cut in 1-inch diagonal
    slices**

In a deep heavy skillet, heat the oil until it is very hot but not smoking. Drop in the plantain slices and brown on all sides. Remove with a slotted spoon, but maintain the oil temperature. Using a *tostonera* (see Glossary) or two pieces of waxed paper, flatten the plantain slices to ¼ inch thick. Refry until golden brown on both sides. Remove and drain on paper towels.

Serves 6

NOTE: For a more sophisticated dish, arrange the *tostones* on a platter and top each with 1 teaspoon of sour cream and ½ teaspoon black or red caviar. Delicious!

Stuffed Tostones
(Tostones Rellenos)

I tried the most delicious stuffed tostones *at Restaurant El Jibarito in Chicago. Carmen, the chef, produces culinary wonders from a very small kitchen!*

STUFFING
- 1 tablespoon annatto oil (see page 8)
- 1 fresh plum tomato, chopped
- 1 tablespoon tomato paste
- 1½ tablespoons Basic *Recaíto* (see page 16)
- ½ pound large shrimp, peeled, cleaned, and diced

- 3 green plantains
- 1 cup corn oil

Heat the annatto oil in a medium skillet. Add the remaining stuffing ingredients. Cook over medium heat for 5 minutes, or until the shrimp turn pink. Set aside. Peel the plantains and cut them into ½-inch rounds. Prepare as for Traditional *Tostones* (see page 39).

Place 1 teaspoon of the shrimp mixture on a *tostón*. Put another *tostón* on top and secure with a toothpick.

Makes 30 stuffed tostones.

NOTE: You can also stuff the *tostones* with seafood salad.

Plantain Chips
(Platanutres)

These have been called Puerto Rican potato chips. They are an excellent party food and are habit forming!

3 **green plantains**
   Ice water
2 **cups corn oil**
   ***Adobo* to taste (see page 15)**

Peel the plantains and slice them paper thin. Place in a bowl of ice water for 20 minutes. Drain and dry the plantain slices. Heat the oil until hot but not smoking and fry the chips briefly, until golden brown and crispy.

Remove from the pan and drain on paper towels. Sprinkle the chips with *adobo*.

Makes about ½ pound

Loíza Crab Burgers
(Tortitas de Cangrejo de Loíza)

The first time I tried crab cakes they were prepared by Rod Avilés, a very talented Puerto Rican chef in New York City. Since I grew up eating crab fritters in Loíza, I thought of them as Loíza crab burgers.

Fresh crumbs made from corn bread or muffins and cilantro give the perfect touch. Serve with fresh avocado slices.

1½ pounds crabmeat
  3 tablespoons mayonnaise
  2 tablespoons Dijon mustard
  2 eggs, beaten
  ½ cup chopped cilantro
  ½ cup fresh, frozen, or canned corn kernels
  1 teaspoon salt
  ½ teaspoon chili powder
  1 cup corn-bread crumbs
  2 cups plain (white) bread crumbs
  ½ tablespoon black pepper
  ¼ cup corn oil

Combine the first 8 ingredients and refrigerate for 30 minutes. Form patties with 2 tablespoons of crab mix for each. Combine the bread crumbs and black pepper on a plate and lightly bread each crab patty. Heat 1 tablespoon of the oil in a skillet and pan-fry the patties until golden brown on each side, adding oil as needed.

Makes 30 crab fritters for hors d'oeuvres; serves 6 to 8 as a main dish

Salt Codfish Fritters
(Bacalaítos)

Fritters are an everyday food on the island. At the fiestas patron-ales, the towns' celebrations to honor their patron saints, street ven-dors offer different versions of this traditional appetizer. This recipe was inspired by the feasts of Cataño, a town located on the north coast, across the bay from Old San Juan.

½ **pound salt *bacalao*, cooked and shredded (see page 8)**
2 **cups all-purpose flour**
1 **teaspoon salt**
½ **teaspoon black pepper**
½ **teaspoon baking powder**
3 **garlic cloves, peeled and chopped**
2 **tablespoons Basic *Recaíto* (see page 16)**
½ **yellow and ½ red bell pepper, seeded and diced**
2 **cups water**
2 **cups corn oil**

Combine the *bacalao*, flour, salt, pepper, baking powder, gar-lic, *recaíto*, and bell pepper in a bowl. Add the water and mix well. Let stand at room temperature for 30 minutes.

Heat the oil in a frying pan until hot but not smoking. Drop the batter by spoonfuls and fry until golden brown on both sides. Drain on paper towels. Keep the fritters warm in a low oven until you finish frying.

Serves 6

Rice-Flour Fritters
(Almojábanas)

This traditional appetizer uses white cheese. These fritters are often served with Mojito Isleño *(see page 21).*

1½ **cups rice flour**
 ½ **cup all-purpose flour**
  2 **teaspoons baking powder**
  1 **teaspoon salt**
  1 **teaspoon black pepper**
 ¾ **cup milk**
  3 **eggs**
 ½ **pound Puerto Rican white cheese, grated**
  3 **cups corn oil**

Combine all of the dry ingredients in a large bowl; add the milk. Beat the eggs into the mixture one at a time. Add the cheese and let the mixture sit at room temperature for at least 2 hours before frying.

Heat the oil in a frying pan until hot but not smoking. Drop the fritters by spoonfuls and fry until golden brown on both sides. Drain on paper towels.

Makes 40 to 45 fritters

Alcapurría

This traditional fritter can also be stuffed with canned corned beef or chicken instead of picadillo.

1¾ pounds *yautía* (taro root)
  3 pounds unripe (green) bananas
  2 teaspoons salt
  3 tablespoons annatto oil (see page 8) plus some to coat
     aluminum foil
  1 recipe Basic Beef *Picadillo* (see page 180)
  2 cups corn oil

Peel the *yautía,* and the green bananas. Grate each vegetable separately on the finest (smallest) side of the grater. Combine the grated vegetables with the salt and annatto oil in a large bowl. Cover with plastic wrap and refrigerate overnight.

Brush a small amount of oil on an 8 × 10-inch square of aluminum foil. Spread on ¼ cup of the dough. Place 1 tablespoon of *picadillo* on top. Fold the foil so the filling is completely covered. Smooth the fritter out with the back of a spoon. Repeat the process with the rest of the dough. When ready to fry, carefully remove the fritters from the foil. In a skillet, heat the corn oil until hot but not smoking. Fry a few *alcapurrías* at a time until golden brown. Drain on paper towels.

Makes 18 alcapurrías.

Shredded Green Plantain Fritters
(Arañitas de Plátano)

Arañitas means "little spiders." Traditionally, this is one of the favorite ways to use plantains on the island. After Hurricane Hugo destroyed many of the plantain fields, these became a gourmet item on island tables.

  6 **tablespoons butter, melted**
  2 **garlic cloves, peeled and chopped**
  1 **tablespoon brandy (optional)**
  3 **medium green plantains, peeled**
    Salt and black pepper to taste
  3 **tablespoons corn or vegetable oil**

Combine 4 tablespoons of the butter with the garlic and brandy and set aside. Coarsely grate the plantains into a bowl and season with the salt and pepper to taste. Heat the oil in a skillet until it is hot but not smoking. Press ¼ cup of the grated plantain at a time in your hands to form a small patty. Fry in the hot oil until golden brown, turning once to make sure it cooks evenly. Repeat with the remaining *arañitas*.

To serve, arrange the *arañitas* on a platter and brush with the remaining melted butter.

Makes 8 to 10 fritters

Meat Turnovers
(Pastelillos de Carne)

Known as empanadas *throughout Latin America,* pastelillos *are street food on the island. Traditional fillings include beef, seafood, and cheese. The small ones are eaten as snacks or appetizers. Larger ones can be a meal with a crisp garden salad.*

1   **pound frozen puff pastry, thawed**
1   **cup Basic Beef** *Picadillo* **(see page 180)**
1   **egg, beaten**

Preheat the oven to 375°F. Roll the dough ⅛ inch thick and cut out circles about 4½ inches wide. Fill one side of each circle with 1½ tablespoons of *picadillo*.

Brush the dough edges with the egg. Fold and press the dough to form a half moon and place on an ungreased cookie sheet. Bake for 30 minutes, or until golden brown.

Makes 10 pastelillos

Rice-Flour Crêpes Stuffed with Shrimp

(Crepas de Harina de Arroz Rellenas de Camarones)

STUFFING
- 1 tablespoon annatto oil
- 1 fresh plum tomato, chopped
- 1 tablespoon tomato paste
- 1½ tablespoons Basic *Recaíto* (see page 16)
- ½ pound large shrimp, cleaned, deveined, and chopped

CRÊPE BATTER
- 1½ cups rice flour
- ½ cup all-purpose flour
- 2 teaspoons baking powder
- ½ teaspoon black pepper
- 1 cup milk
- 3 eggs
- ½ pound Puerto Rican white cheese, grated
- Olive oil for frying

Heat the annatto oil in a large skillet. Add the plum tomato, tomato paste, and *recaíto*. Cook over medium heat for 3 minutes. Stir in the shrimp and cook until they just turn pink. Set aside.

Sift the dry ingredients together. With a wooden spoon, slowly stir in the milk, then the eggs. Continue stirring until the mixture is smooth and free of lumps. Add the grated cheese. Let the batter rest for 1 hour in the refrigerator.

Heat a 7-inch frying pan and coat it with 1 tablespoon of olive oil. Pour in ¼ cup of the crêpe batter and cook briefly, until golden brown on one side. Turn the crêpe over and cook for 1 minute. Repeat the process, adding more oil as needed, with the remaining batter.

To assemble the crêpes, place 2 teaspoons of the stuffing on one side of each crêpe. Lift the edges and roll. Secure with a toothpick. Serve at room temperature or rewarm in a very low oven.

Makes 15 to 20 crêpes

Cornsticks
(Sorullitos de Maíz)

The most famous cornsticks come from La Parguera, the phosphorescent bay located on the southwest coast. They are served with a sauce made from ketchup and mayonnaise known as Sauce Andaluse.

    2 cups water
    1 teaspoon salt or *Adobo* (see page 15)
 1½ cups yellow cornmeal
    ½ cup grated Cheddar cheese
    3 cups corn oil

Bring the water and salt to a boil in a small saucepan. Add the cornmeal. Reduce the heat to low and cook, stirring constantly, for 3 to 5 minutes, until thickened. Remove the pot from the heat and add the grated cheese. Let the mixture cool a little. Shape 2 tablespoons of dough into a stick about 3 inches long. Repeat with the remaining dough. Heat the oil in a skillet until hot but not smoking and fry until golden brown on all sides.

Makes 18 to 20 sticks

NOTE: You can also use Parmesan, Edam, or white cheese.

Chicken "Cracklings"
(*Chicharrones de Pollo*)

The word chicharrón *makes me think right away of the famous pork cracklings sold by street vendors in Bayamón, a town on the north coast of the island.*

   In this case it refers to one of our most famous traditional dishes, small pieces of chicken that are crispy on the outside but very moist and tender inside. This recipe was inspired by Rosa Franco, the owner of a small factory that manufactures flanes (*custards*) *in Connecticut.*

1   3½-pound chicken, cut in small pieces
     Salt, black pepper, and dried oregano to taste
3   garlic cloves, peeled and chopped
½   cup golden rum
     Juice of 3 lemons
1   cup all-purpose flour
2   teaspoons salt
2   teaspoons black pepper
¼   cup corn oil

   Sprinkle the chicken with salt, pepper, oregano, and garlic. Marinate in the rum and lemon juice for 30 minutes. Drain. In a plastic bag, combine the flour with the salt and pepper and dredge the chicken pieces, shaking off the excess. Heat the oil in a large skillet until hot but not smoking and fry the chicken pieces, a few at a time, until all sides are golden brown. Serve at once.

Serves 6

NOTE: You can use brandy instead of rum.

5

SOUPS
(Sopas)

Our national soup is *asopao* (chicken soup). Most traditional soups, somewhere between soups and stews, are based on a combination of assorted root vegetables, meats, and a *sofrito*-based sauce.

New soups, like sauces, use fruits as main ingredients. Cream soups have also resulted from the new trends. Cold soups, very appropriate for the warm climate, have now become quite popular.

Chicken Soup
(Asopao de Pollo)

Our national soup asopao *is a medley of chicken, rice, and season-ings that nourishes the body and soul.*

During the Christmas season, when groups of family and friends get together at the asaltos *(singing Christmas carols from house to house), the best way to end the evening is with a big pot of steaming* asopao. *Not only is it great party food, but it tastes better when re-heated the next day.*

1 **3-pound chicken, cut into serving pieces**
   Adobo **to taste (see page 15)**
3 **tablespoons annatto oil**
4 **ounces smoked ham, diced**
½ **cup Basic** *Recaíto* **(see page 16)**
1 **cup tomato sauce**
½ **cup** *alcaparrado*
6 **cups water**
2 **cups short-grain rice**
2 **teaspoons salt**
1 **teaspoon black pepper**
½ **cup green peas, cooked, for garnish**
½ **cup diced pimientos for garnish**

Season the chicken with the *adobo*. Set aside. Heat the oil in a large soup pot and sauté the ham over medium heat. Add the *recaíto*, tomato sauce, and *alcaparrado*. Cook for 5 minutes.

Add the chicken and water, and bring to a boil. Stir in the rice, salt, and pepper, and turn the heat to medium-low. Cover and simmer for 30 minutes, or until the rice is done.

The soup should have a thick consistency. Serve in bowls and garnish with the peas and pimientos.

Serves 6 to 8

NOTE: If you want to prepare this soup for a party, double the recipe. For a new twist you can add blanched broccoli florets. You can also make *asopao* with shrimp, lobster, or salt codfish, instead of chicken.

Puerto Rican Chicken Noodle Soup
(Sopa de Fideos y Pollo)

This is another Puerto Rican version of the cure-all soup. It is one of the first solid foods given to babies, as well as the classic remedy for colds.

 2 pounds boneless chicken breast, cut into pieces
   Adobo to taste (see page 15)
 8 cups chicken stock
 ½ cup Basic *Recaíto* (see page 16)
 4 ounces angel hair pasta, crushed
 1¼ pounds potatoes, peeled and diced
 ¼ cup short-grain rice
 2 teaspoons salt, or to taste
 2 teaspoons black pepper
 2 sprigs cilantro

Season the chicken with the *adobo*. Bring the chicken, water, and *recaíto* to a boil in a soup kettle. Add the remaining ingredients and bring to another boil. Reduce the heat to low and cook for 20 minutes, or until the rice and noodles are cooked.

Serves 6 to 8

Green Pigeon Pea Soup
(*Asopao de Gandules*)

This is a variation of our national soup, asopao de pollo. *For vegetarians, like my friend Judith Velez, this soup, made with water instead of stock, is a real treat.*

My mother used to pick fresh gandules *pods from the beautiful trees in our backyard. I would gather the* recao, *sweet chili peppers, and cilantro for her. My father's job was to shell and pick over the green pigeon peas.*

- **1   14-ounce package frozen *gandules* (green pigeon peas), thawed**
- **2   quarts chicken stock or water**
- **2   tablespoons light olive oil**
- **½   medium red onion, chopped**
- **½   red bell pepper, seeded and chopped**
- **2   sweet chili peppers, seeded and diced**
- **3   *recao* leaves, minced, or 2 tablespoons chopped cilantro**
- **2   garlic cloves, peeled and minced**
- **1   cup tomato sauce**
- **2   cups short-grain rice**
- **1   pound West Indian pumpkin, peeled and diced**
- **½   tablespoon salt, or to taste**
- **⅓   cup chopped cilantro**

In a large pot or soup kettle, combine the *gandules* and 2 cups of the stock. Cook until tender, about 20 minutes. Drain and set aside. Heat the oil in a skillet. Add the onion, bell pepper, chili pepper, *recao*, garlic, and tomato sauce. Sauté over medium heat for 5 minutes.

Combine the *gandules*, tomato mixture, rice, pumpkin, salt, and the remaining stock in a soup pot. Bring to a boil; lower the heat and simmer for 25 minutes, or until the rice is cooked and the soup has thickened. Add the cilantro just before serving.

Serves 6

57

Chicken Broth with Plantain "Dumplings"

(Caldo de Pollo con Bolitas de Plátano)

Green bok choy leaves make an unexpected garnish for this everyday peasant dish.

- 1 **large green plantain, peeled and shredded through the next-to-finest side of the grater**
- 10 **cups chicken stock**
- ½ **tablespoon salt**
- ½ **tablespoon black pepper**
- 1 **cup bok choy leaves cut in very thin strips**

Form dumplings from ½ tablespoonfuls of shredded plantain and set aside. Bring the chicken broth to a boil in a large pot. Add the salt, pepper, and dumplings. Reduce the heat to medium-low and cook for 15 minutes. Add the bok choy and cook for another 5 minutes.

Serves 6 to 8

Plantain Soup Creole Style
(*Sopa de Plátanos Estilo Criollísimo*)

I had this soup at Criollísimo, one of the finest restaurants in San Juan. Giovanna Huyke, island cooking teacher and television personality, arranged a tasting menu for me. We both agreed that this soup, although very easy to prepare, is packed with flavor.

6 cups chicken stock
2 green plantains, peeled and coarsely grated
1 small yellow onion, chopped
1 tablespoon annatto oil (see page 8)
3 garlic cloves, minced
Salt and black pepper to taste

Combine all of the ingredients in a large soup pot and bring to a simmer. Reduce the heat to low and cook, stirring occasionally, until the plantain is tender, about 20 minutes.

Serves 6

Gallician Soup
(Caldo Gallego)

This soup from Spain has become as much a part of our culinary tradition as roast suckling pig.

- 8 cups chicken stock or water
- ½ pound white navy beans, cooked
- ½ pound smoked ham, diced
- 2 *chorizos* (red Spanish sausages), sliced
- 1 medium yellow onion, sliced
- 3 garlic cloves, peeled and chopped
- 1 pound potatoes, peeled and diced
- 1 10-ounce box frozen collard greens, thawed
  Salt and black pepper to taste

Combine all of the ingredients in a large soup pot and bring to a boil. Lower the heat and simmer for 30 minutes.

Serves 6 to 8

White Bean Soup
(*Sopa de Habichuelas Blancas*)

I had a nanny, Delfa, who used to make this delicious soup. At lunch-time I would run home from school and find her waiting for me with a steaming bowl of bright red soup filled with white beans and chunks of salami.

  1 **tablespoon annatto oil (see page 8)**
  4 **ounces fresh bacon, diced**
  4 **ounces Genoa salami, diced**
  ¼ **cup Basic *Recaíto* (see page 16)**
  ½ **cup manzanilla olives, chopped**
  1 **cup tomato sauce**
  ½ **pound white navy beans, cooked**
  8 **cups water**
  ¼ **cup short-grain rice**
  2 **ounces angel hair pasta or fidellini**
  ½ **tablespoon salt**
  1 **teaspoon black pepper**

Heat the oil in a heavy skillet and sauté the bacon and salami. Add the *recaíto*, olives, and tomato sauce. Cook over medium heat for 3 minutes.

In a soup kettle, combine the beans and water. Add the bacon mixture, rice, noodles, and salt and pepper. Bring the soup to a boil, then reduce the heat and simmer for 20 minutes, or until the rice is cooked.

Serves 6 to 8

Tripe Soup
(Mondongo)

A soup to cure anything! Adela Fargas of Casa Adela in New York is famous for her mondongo.

- 2 pounds honeycomb tripe, cut into small pieces
- 4 cups lemon juice combined with 8 cups cold water
- 3 quarts cold water mixed with 1 tablespoon salt
- 1 tablespoon annatto oil (see page 8)
- 1 tablespoon corn oil
- ¼ pound smoked ham, diced
- ½ cup Basic *Recaíto* (see page 16)
- 1 cup tomato sauce
- 1 cup *alcaparrado*
- ½ pound each *yautía* (taro root), *yuca* (cassava), and *calabaza* (West Indian pumpkin), all peeled and diced
- 1 green plantain, peeled and sliced
- 4 bay leaves
- ½ tablespoon black pepper
- Salt to taste

Soak the tripe in the lemon water for 30 minutes. Rinse and put in a large soup pot with the 3 quarts of cold salted water. Bring to a boil. Lower the heat, cover, and simmer for about 2½ hours, or until the tripe is tender. Drain and rinse.

In a clean pot, heat the oils. Add the ham, *recaíto*, tomato sauce, and *alcaparrado*. Sauté over medium heat for 5 minutes. Add the tripe, root vegetables, plantain, bay leaves, and enough cold water to cover. Add pepper and salt. Bring to a boil, reduce the heat, and simmer for 40 minutes, or until the root vegetables are cooked.

Serves 10 to 15

NOTE: You can also add 1 cup drained canned garbanzos (chick-peas) to taste. Add them 5 minutes before serving.

Assorted Root-Vegetable Soup
(Sancocho)

Sancocho, *a classic stew, is like a tropical still life. It is a combination of root vegetables, tubers, plantains, and meats. Meats can vary from beef and pork to chicken. Traditionally served with white rice,* sancocho *is a meal in itself. It is ideal for cold days of winter. Serve it with garlic bread and a tossed salad.*

2 pounds short ribs of beef
¼ pound smoked ham, diced
4 quarts chicken stock or water
½ cup Basic *Recaíto* (see page 16)
1 cup tomato sauce
1 pound each *calabaza* (West Indian pumpkin), *yautía* (taro root), *apio, ñame* (yam), and *yuca* (cassava), peeled and diced in 1-inch cubes
2 medium green plantains, peeled and cut in 2-inch pieces
3 ears fresh corn, cut into 1-inch pieces
1 tablespoon salt
1 tablespoon black pepper
1 quart water

In a big soup pot, combine the first 6 ingredients, including all the root vegetables. Cover and bring to a boil. Reduce the heat to medium, cover, and simmer for 30 minutes.

Add the remaining ingredients and bring to another boil. Lower the heat and simmer, covered, for 45 minutes, or until the vegetables are cooked. Adjust the seasonings.

Serves 10 to 12

Caldo Santo

This soup is typical of Loíza Aldea, a town located on the east coast, where our African heritage is predominant. A lot of coconut-based dishes originated here.

Caldo Santo is eaten during Holy Week. My friend Evelyn Collazo described this soup to me while we were viewing an art exhibit at the Museo del Barrio in New York City. We daydreamed about an open fire near the beach and the sweet fragrance of coconut milk and root vegetables on the breeze.

7   cups coconut milk
½   cup annatto seeds
1   cup Basic *Recaíto* (see page 16)
3   quarts water
1   cup *alcaparrado* or manzanilla olives
1   pound each *yuca* (cassava), *yautía* (taro root), *batata* (Puerto Rican sweet potato), *calabaza* (West Indian pumpkin), and *ñame* (yam), peeled and cut into 1-inch cubes
2   green plantains, peeled and shredded, shaped into 1-inch balls (12 to 14 balls)
     Salt to taste
1   pound medium shrimp, peeled and cleaned
1   pound *bacalao* (salt codfish), cooked and shredded (see page 8)
8   blue crabs
1   pound boneless fillet of red snapper, cut into pieces

Heat 1 cup of the coconut milk with the annatto seeds. When the milk turns bright red, remove it from the heat and strain. Set the milk aside and discard the seeds. In a big soup pot, combine the annatto-colored milk, the remaining coconut milk, and the *recaíto*. Bring to a simmer. Add the water, *alcaparrado*, root vegetables, and plantain balls. Add the salt and bring to a boil. Add all the seafood and simmer for 30 minutes, or until the root vegetables are cooked. Let the soup cool a little before serving.

Serves 8 to 10

Chayote Seafood Chowder
(Sopa de Chayote y Mariscos)

Chayote, *a tropical squash shaped like a pear, has a mild flavor and a firm, crunchy texture.* Chayote *is low in calories and is a good source of potassium. Combined with seafood, it produces a delicate chowder with a tropical touch.*

2 medium *chayotes*, peeled and diced
2 celery stalks, cut into small pieces
2 carrots, peeled and diced
5 cups chicken stock or water
1 cup fresh, frozen, or canned corn kernels
1 cup light cream
½ pound medium shrimp, peeled and cleaned
12 clams, in shells, cleaned
12 mussels, in shells, cleaned
½ cup golden rum (optional)
3 cups water
3 sprigs cilantro
1 teaspoon salt
White pepper to taste
Pimiento strips for garnish

In a large soup pot, combine the *chayote,* celery, carrot, and chicken stock. Bring to a boil, reduce the heat, and simmer for 30 minutes. Let cool a little, then purée in a blender. Add the corn and cream and set aside.

Combine the seafood, rum, water, and cilantro in a large pot. Cover and cook briefly until the shrimp turn pink and the shellfish open up. Drain and combine with the *chayote* mixture. Return to the stove, add the salt and pepper, and simmer until hot, but do not boil. Garnish with pimiento strips.

Serves 6

Cold Taro Root Soup
(Sopa Fría de Yautía)

While doing my culinary apprenticeship with Joe Kugler, a French chef, I learned to prepare cold leek-and-potato soup. I grew up eating viandas *(root vegetables), so I immediately adapted this classic dish using* yautía *(taro root).*

2½ pounds *yautía* (taro root), peeled and diced
2 medium yellow onions, sliced
4 cups chicken stock or canned broth
1 cup light cream
1 teaspoon salt
1 teaspoon white pepper
Pinch ground nutmeg

Cook the *yautía* with the yellow onion in the chicken stock for 30 minutes, or until tender. Drain. Purée the mixture in a blender or food processor and strain through a sieve. Add the remaining ingredients.

Refrigerate for 2 hours before serving.

Serves 6

NOTE: This soup is also good hot or at room temperature.

Cold Avocado Soup La Fortaleza

(Sopa Fría de Aguacate Estilo La Fortaleza)

Although we have summer weather throughout the year in Puerto Rico, cold soups are not an everyday food. When the former governor, Carlos Romero Barceló, took over La Fortaleza (the Governor's mansion) in 1981, he served a cold avocado soup at the opening-ceremony lunch. The soup became an instant hit in the best restaurants in San Juan.

> 4 medium avocados, peeled and diced
> ½ cup plain yogurt
> ½ cup light cream
> 2 cups chicken stock
> Juice of 3 lemons
> Salt and white pepper to taste
> 2 or 3 plum tomatoes, roughly chopped, for garnish
> 2 tablespoons watercress, roughly chopped, for garnish

Combine all of the ingredients except the tomato and watercress in a blender or food processor and process until very smooth. Season to taste. Chill for at least 1 hour before serving. Garnish with tomato and watercress.

Serves 6 to 8

Papaya and Garlic Soup
(Sopa de Papaya y Ajo)

On a trip to the island, I discovered a papaya tree in my father's back-yard, full of beautifully ripe fruit. I had a great time figuring out ways to use all those papayas. Sipping some freshly squeezed orange juice, I came up with this simple and flavorful soup.

4   garlic cloves, peeled and sliced
1   cup fresh orange juice
3   cups chicken stock
4   papayas, peeled and cut into 1-inch dice
1   cup light cream
3   tablespoons sugar
    Fresh mint leaves for garnish

In a skillet, combine the garlic with the orange juice and chicken stock. Simmer until the garlic is tender, about 20 minutes. Let the mixture cool to room temperature. Purée the papaya with the orange-juice mixture in a blender or food processor and pass it through a sieve. Transfer the mixture to a bowl and whisk in the cream and sugar. Garnish with mint leaves.

Serves 6 to 8

NOTE: This soup can be served at room temperature or chilled.

Cold Mango and Rum Soup
(Sopa Fría de Mango y Ron)

On the island mangoes are in season from February until August. Here they are a real summer joy. This soup can be served as an appetizer or to end a Sunday brunch.

5 **medium mangoes, peeled and cut into small pieces**
1 **cup coconut milk**
1 **cup milk**
½ **teaspoon ground cinnamon**
3 **tablespoons honey**
3 **tablespoons golden rum**
 Freshly grated nutmeg for garnish

Purée the mango in a blender or food processor, then pass through a sieve. Combine the mango purée with the remaining ingredients except the nutmeg. Garnish with the nutmeg.

Serves 6

West Indian Pumpkin and Apple Soup

(Sopa de Calabaza y Manzana)

This is my Puerto Rican version of a delicious soup prepared by Waldy Malouf, chef at the Hudson River Club in New York.

- 3 pounds *calabaza* (West Indian pumpkin), peeled, seeded, and cubed
- 4 green apples, peeled, seeded, and coarsely chopped
- 1 medium yellow onion, diced
- 1 Italian frying pepper, seeded and diced
- 2 sweet chili peppers, seeded
- 6 cups chicken broth
- ½ tablespoon salt
  White pepper to taste
  Chopped cilantro and ground nutmeg for garnish

Combine all of the ingredients except the cilantro and nutmeg in a large soup pot and bring to a boil. Lower the heat and simmer for 20 minutes. Drain any excess liquid and purée in a blender. Adjust the seasonings. Rewarm the soup over medium heat. Garnish with cilantro and nutmeg.

Serves 8

6

SALADS AND VEGETABLE DISHES
(Ensaladas y Platos a Base de Vegetales)

Although we are not big salad eaters, some salads, such as *chayote* and potato, are basic to our traditional cooking.

There are also dishes resulting from the Puerto Rican New Cuisine. Beans, used traditionally in stews, are now combined with other vegetables. These new bean salads in some cases replace traditional rice and beans as side dishes.

Pasta salads have become very popular, too. Avocado is combined with seafood in light main-dish selections. Overall, salads and vegetable dishes have become a larger part of our daily diet than ever before.

Chayote Salad
(Ensalada de Chayote)

The firm, moist flesh of chayote *is ideal for salads and vegetable dishes. Cubes of* chayote *are good with chicken, pork, or seafood. For a main-dish salad just toss* chayote *with avocado slices and a light vinaigrette. I also like to serve it with Ajilimójili Sauce (see page 19) or the dressings that follow.*

4 medium *chayotes*
1 6-ounce jar pimientos, drained and diced

Peel the *chayotes* and cut each into 4 pieces. Boil in enough salted water to cover for 20 minutes, or until tender. Let cool at room temperature. Add a dressing and toss gently.

Serves 6

CILANTRO VINAIGRETTE
    3 tablespoons olive oil
    1 tablespoon vinegar
    1 tablespoon chopped cilantro
       Salt and black pepper to taste

SHERRY VINAIGRETTE
    ¼ cup sherry vinegar
    1 tablespoon Dijon mustard
    1 cup olive oil
       Salt and black pepper to taste

CITRUS VINAIGRETTE
    ¼ cup fresh lemon juice
    ¼ cup fresh orange juice
    2 tablespoons fresh orange peel
    1 cup olive oil
       Salt and black pepper to taste

TOMATO AND BASIL DRESSING

2 tomatoes, chopped
¼ cup chopped fresh basil
¼ cup cider vinegar
1 cup olive oil

Traditional Green Salad
(Ensalada Verde Tradicional)

No meal on the island is complete without a bowl of this salad. Red-tipped curly lettuce can be used instead of green. My mother used to drizzle on just a touch of oil, vinegar, and salt. You can use white-wine vinegar or a fruit vinegar such as raspberry.

3 cups curly green lettuce, cleaned and cut in thin strips
2 medium tomatoes, sliced
1 cucumber, peeled, seeded, and diced
1 cup cooked or canned corn kernels
1 cup green peas, cooked and chilled
1 6-ounce jar pimientos, drained and cut in strips, for garnish

Combine all of the ingredients except the pimientos in a serving bowl. Garnish with the pimientos.

Serves 6

Mom's Potato Salad
(Ensalada de Papa de Mami)

Summer vacations meant countless trips to the beach. The whole family would plan the menu, and my mom always prepared this potato salad.

3 pounds potatoes, peeled, diced, and cooked
1 cup mayonnaise
1 medium yellow onion, chopped
1 green bell pepper, seeded and chopped
4 eggs, hard-cooked and roughly chopped
2 medium apples, peeled, cored, and diced
1 6-ounce jar pimientos, drained and cut into strips
½ cup green peas, cooked, for garnish

Combine all of the ingredients except the peas in a serving bowl. Garnish with the peas.

Serves 8 to 10

Green Beans in Garlic Vinaigrette
(Habichuelas Tiernas con Vinagreta de Ajo)

While I was in college, Luis Loyola, a dear friend, prepared this salad for me and my roommate Mabel. You can use fresh green beans, so abundant in the summer months. I have added chopped black olives as a garnish.

1½ pounds green beans, cleaned and cut into 2-inch
     pieces
6 garlic cloves, peeled
3 sweet chili peppers, seeded
¼ cup white vinegar
¾ cup olive oil
1 teaspoon salt
1 teaspoon black pepper
⅓ cup chopped black olives for garnish

Blanch the green beans in boiling water for 3 to 5 minutes. Drain and cool. In a mortar, crush the garlic and sweet chili peppers. Transfer them to a bowl and add the vinegar, oil, salt, and pepper. Toss the beans with the dressing. Garnish with the olives.

Serves 6

Green Pigeon Pea and Carrot Salad
(Ensalada de Gandules y Zanahorias)

Edgar Sanchez, my son's godfather, is an excellent cook. He served this salad at Alex's christening party.

  2 **14-ounce bags frozen *gandules* (green pigeon peas) (or 2 14-ounce cans, drained)**
  2 **quarts chicken stock or water**
  2 **pounds carrots, peeled and diced**
  ½ **cup cider vinegar**
1½ **cups olive oil**
  1 **yellow onion, sliced**
  1 **yellow bell pepper, seeded and sliced**
  3 **bay leaves**
  1 **teaspoon salt**
  1 **teaspoon black pepper**
  ½ **teaspoon dried oregano**

Cook the *gandules* in the chicken stock for 20 minutes, or until tender. Drain and cool. Blanch the carrots in boiling water for about 5 minutes. Drain and cool. Combine the remaining ingredients and add the *gandules* and carrots. Let the salad marinate for at least 2 hours in the refrigerator, or better, overnight.

Serves 6 to 8

Green Pigeon Pea and Orzo Salad
(Ensalada de Gandules y Orzo)

Orzo (rice-shaped pasta) combined with gandules *(green pigeon peas) makes a pretty variation of the rice–and–*gandules *dish. Yellow peppers add the perfect touch.*

1 cup orzo, cooked according to package instructions
1 16-ounce can *gandules* (green pigeon peas), drained
1 medium yellow bell pepper, seeded and diced
1 medium red onion, sliced
¼ cup red wine vinegar
1 cup sunflower oil
2 teaspoons salt
1 teaspoon black pepper
3 tablespoons chopped cilantro

Combine the orzo, *gandules*, yellow pepper, and onion in a large bowl. In another bowl, whisk the oil into the vinegar and add the salt and pepper. Pour the dressing over the salad. Add the cilantro and toss well. Refrigerate for at least 30 minutes before serving.

Serves 6 to 8

Avocado and Tomato Salad
(*Ensalada de Aguacate y Tomate*)

This simple salad is usually served with viandas *(root vegetables)* and bacalao *(salt cod).*

- 1 **large avocado, peeled and sliced**
- 1 **pound plum tomatoes, sliced**
- 1 **medium yellow onion, sliced**
  Cider vinegar and olive oil to taste
- 2 **teaspoons salt**
- 2 **teaspoons black pepper**
  Dash hot sauce (optional)

Combine all of the ingredients in a nonreactive bowl.

Serves 6

VARIATION: For an interesting twist add a papaya, peeled and diced. You can also substitute a red onion for the yellow.

Rice Salad
(Ensalada de Arroz)

During my last year in college a group of friends got together for Thanksgiving. It was my first potluck dinner. Lourdes Morales, a classmate, prepared a rice salad. She used bottled Italian dressing, but I prefer a fresh garlic-and-cilantro vinaigrette.

- 2 cups cooked rice
- 2 cups frozen mixed vegetables, cooked
- 2 tablespoons olive oil
- 1 medium yellow onion, chopped
- 1 medium red bell pepper, seeded and chopped
- 1 garlic clove, peeled and chopped
- ⅓ cup loosely packed cilantro
- ⅓ cup olive oil
- 1½ tablespoons cider vinegar
- 1 teaspoon salt

Combine the rice and mixed vegetables in a large bowl. Set aside. Heat the oil in a skillet and sauté the onion and pepper until golden brown. Let cool to room temperature. Combine the garlic, cilantro, oil, and vinegar in a blender or food processor; add the salt, and set aside. Add the onion and pepper to the rice mixture. Pour the dressing over the salad and toss.

Serves 6

Sautéed Chayotes
(Chayotes Salteados)

Get away from the meat-and-potatoes routine with this light and delicious side dish.

3 medium *chayotes*, peeled and sliced
1 tablespoon butter
1 tablespoon corn oil
1 teaspoon salt
    Black pepper

Blanch the *chayote* slices in boiling water for 2 minutes. Drain and set aside.

Heat the butter and oil. Add the *chayote* and sauté over high heat until it turns lightly golden. Sprinkle with salt and pepper.

Serves 6

NOTE: Sprinkle toasted pine nuts on top for a tasty garnish.

Chayote Hash
(Boronía de Chayote)

This hash can be served for brunch with breakfast sausages or ham.

3 quarts water
1 tablespoon salt
4 medium *chayotes*, peeled and diced
1 tablespoon annatto oil (see page 8)
3 eggs, beaten
2 tablespoons tomato sauce
½ tablespoon Basic *Recaíto* (see page 16)
  Salt and black pepper to taste

In a large pot, bring the water to a boil. Add the salt and the *chayote* and cook for 20 minutes. Drain and set aside. Heat the oil in a skillet. Add the eggs and cook over medium heat until they are slightly set. Add the tomato sauce, *recaíto*, and *chayote*. Cook for 5 more minutes, stirring constantly, or until the eggs are completely cooked.

Serves 6

Stuffed Chayotes
(Chayotes Rellenos)

This dish is a meal in itself. Serve it with a green salad.

3 large *chayotes*
1 tablespoon annatto oil (see page 8) or olive oil
4 ounces smoked ham, cut into small cubes
½ cup manzanilla olives, chopped
¼ cup Basic *Recaíto* (see page 16) combined with ¼ cup
    tomato sauce or 3 tablespoons tomato paste
1 pound ground beef
2 eggs, beaten
½ cup plain bread crumbs
    Parmesan cheese to taste (optional)

Cut the *chayotes* in half and cook them in a large pot of boiling water for 30 minutes. Drain and cool. Heat the oil in a heavy skillet. Sauté the ham, olives, *recaíto* or tomato paste, and ground beef over medium heat. Scoop the pulp out of the *chayotes*, chop, and add to the meat stuffing.

Preheat the oven to 375°F. Fill each *chayote* shell with the meat mixture. Top each shell with eggs and bread crumbs and sprinkle with cheese. Bake for 10 minutes, or until the egg has set.

Serves 6

NOTE: You can also use equal parts of ground beef and veal or veal and pork.

Stuffed Italian Frying Peppers
(Pimientos de Cocinar Rellenos)

This is an adaptation of the all-American dish, stuffed bell peppers.

1½ tablespoons annatto oil (see page 8)
2 tablespoons Basic *Recaíto* (see page 16)
½ cup *gandules* (green pigeon peas)
½ cup tomato sauce
1½ cups converted long-grain rice
2 cups boiling water or chicken stock
¼ cup dried currants
1 teaspoon salt
1 teaspoon black pepper
6 Italian frying peppers (if possible get them all the same size)
1 tablespoon olive oil

Heat the annatto oil in a saucepan. Add the *recaíto, gandules,* and tomato sauce and sauté over medium heat for 5 minutes. Add the rice, water, currants, and seasonings. Bring the mixture to a boil, and cook over medium-high heat until the liquid evaporates. Reduce the heat to low and stir. Cook, covered, for 20 minutes, stirring after 10 minutes.

Preheat the oven to 375°F. Cut the peppers on the top and remove any seeds. Stuff each with 3 tablespoons of the rice mixture. Grease a baking pan with the olive oil. Arrange the peppers in the pan and bake for 40 minutes. Serve each pepper with ½ cup of the remaining rice.

Serves 6

Stewed Okra
(*Quimbombó Guisado*)

Okra is my father's favorite vegetable. A gift from the African continent, it is a staple vegetable in traditional Puerto Rican cooking.

½ **pound fatback, diced, or 6 slices bacon, chopped**
1 **cup sliced yellow onion**
1 **pound fresh plum tomatoes, seeded and chopped**
½ **cup Basic *Recaíto* (see page 16) combined with 1 cup tomato sauce**
1½ **pounds fresh okra, tips trimmed**
½ **cup chicken stock or water**

Sauté the fatback or bacon in a Dutch oven over medium-high heat. Discard the excess fat. Add the onion, tomato, and *recaíto* mixture. Bring to a boil and cook for 5 minutes. Add the okra and chicken stock. Bring to another boil. Reduce the heat and simmer for 15 minutes, or until the okra is cooked.

Serves 4 to 6

VARIATION: You can add 2 fresh ears of corn, cut into 1-inch pieces, when you add the okra.

Puerto Rican Polenta
(Funche Puertorriqueño)

Funche, *a staple in the Taíno diet is known in Italy as polenta and in the American south as cornmeal mush.* Funche *can be sweet or savory. Cooked with milk and sugar, it is served for breakfast or dessert. As a side dish it is classically combined with beans.*

- 2 tablespoons butter
- 6 cups water
- 1 tablespoon salt
- 2 cups yellow cornmeal
  Butter for greasing the baking pan

Bring the butter, water, and salt to a boil in a large pot. Whisk in the cornmeal, stirring constantly. Reduce the heat to medium-low and continue to cook, stirring constantly for 15 minutes, or until the *funche* is thick enough to hold its shape. Pour into a greased 9-inch square baking pan. Let it cool for 5 minutes before slicing.

Serves 6 to 8

Polenta Gnocchi
(Gnocchi de Funche)

A creative way to serve funche.

1 recipe Puerto Rican Polenta (see page 88)
1 tablespoon olive oil
½ recipe tomato sauce used for cannelloni (see page 180)
1 cup shredded mozzarella

Prepare the polenta as in Puerto Rican Polenta, but pour it into a sheet pan with sides (a jelly roll pan will work) and let cool.

Preheat the oven to 350°F. Cut the polenta into 1-inch circles with a cookie cutter. Grease a large shallow baking pan with olive oil. Arrange the polenta circles and cover them with the tomato sauce and mozzarella.

Bake for 30 minutes, or until the cheese has melted.

Serves 8

Puerto Rican Tamales
(Guanimes)

Corn tamales were another staple in the Taíno diet. In traditional cooking they were served with salt codfish stew. If banana leaves are not available, you can use parchment paper or aluminum foil. You'll also need butcher's twine, for tying.

1	**pound yellow cornmeal**
¼	**cup all-purpose flour**
2	**cups milk**
2	**cinnamon sticks**
1	**teaspoon salt**
10 to 12	**plantain or banana leaves, or parchment paper**
3	**quarts salted water**

Combine the dry ingredients in a large bowl. In a small saucepan bring the milk, cinnamon sticks, and salt to a boil. Remove the cinnamon sticks and add the milk slowly to the dry ingredients. Mix until the liquid is absorbed.

Cut the plantain leaves in pieces large enough to wrap ¼ cup of the dough in each (about 8 × 8 inches). Put the dough in the center of a plantain leaf. Fold up the sides and ends and tie with butcher's twine. Repeat until all of the corn mixture has been used.

Bring the salted water to a boil in a very large pot. Add the *guanimes* and simmer for 1 hour. To serve, unwrap the *guanimes* and place on a platter. Serve with Salt Codfish Stew or *Mojito Isleño* (see pages 119 and 21).

Makes 10 to 12 guanimes

7

Plantains, Root Vegetables, and Tubers
(Viandas)

All root vegetables can be cooked by steaming or boiling. In traditional dishes they are usually fried, however. New dishes include stuffed *mofongo* (plantain dumplings), *yuca* (cassava), vegetarian chili, and sautéed yellow plantain with Parmesan cheese.

Viandas are also eaten as a side dish instead of rice and beans. Since root vegetables are high in complex carbohydrates, they are healthy options in today's recommended diet.

Basic Fried Yellow Plantains
(Maduros Fritos)

Fried yellow plantains, like green ones, are staple everyday side dishes. They are also served for breakfast with eggs and Vienna sausages.

1 cup corn oil
3 yellow plantains, peeled and cut into 2-inch slices

Heat the oil in a skillet and fry the plantain slices until golden brown on all sides.

Serves 6

Baked Yellow Plantains
(*Maduros Asados*)

In the old days, cooks would roast plantains over el fogón (an open fire). You can do it in the oven. It is easier, although not as much fun as it used to be.

6 medium yellow plantains
4 tablespoons olive oil
   Salt to taste

Preheat the oven to 400°F. Cut a 2-inch slit in each plantain and wrap with aluminum foil. Bake for 40 minutes. Peel the plantains and arrange them on a serving platter. Drizzle olive oil over all and season with salt.

Serves 6

Yellow Plantain and Meat Pie
(Pastelón de Amarillos)

The mozzarella cheese adds an Italian touch to this Puerto Rican version of lasagna.

FILLING

- 1 pound ground beef
- 5 plum tomatoes, seeded and diced
- ½ cup Basic *Recaíto* (see page 16)
- ½ cup manzanilla olives, chopped
- ½ cup golden raisins
- 1 cup tomato sauce
- 1 teaspoon salt
- 1 teaspoon dried oregano
- ½ tablespoon black pepper

"DOUGH"

- 2 cups corn oil
- 7 very ripe yellow plantains, peeled and cut into 3-inch slices
- ½ pound mozzarella cheese, shredded

TOPPING

- ½ pound green beans, cooked
- 6 eggs, beaten

Brown the meat in a large frying pan. Add the remaining filling ingredients and cook over medium heat for 5 minutes. Set aside.

Preheat the oven to 350°F. Heat the oil and fry the plantain until golden brown. Drain on paper towels.

Spread ½ cup of the filling in the bottom of a 9-inch square baking pan. Add a layer of half of the plantain slices and cover with the remaining filling. Add the mozzarella cheese. Top with the remaining plantain slices. Sprinkle the green beans on top and pour the eggs over all. Bake for 45 minutes, or until the eggs are set.

Serves 12 to 15

Yellow Plantain Boats Stuffed with Beef Picadillo
(Canoas de Plátano Relleno de Carne)

This was one of my favorite lunchtime dishes at Restaurante El Roble in Río Piedras. A whole plantain makes a main dish; pieces of stuffed plantain "boats" are lovely as a side dish.

- 2 **cups corn oil**
- 6 **ripe but firm yellow plantains, peeled**
- 1 **recipe Beef** *Picadillo* **(see page 180)**
- ¼ **pound Cheddar cheese, shredded**

Preheat the oven to 350°F. Heat the oil in a frying pan and fry the plantains until golden brown. Drain on paper towels. Make a slit in each plantain from top to bottom. Fill each with 2½ tablespoons of the *picadillo*. Sprinkle the cheese on top. Bake for 15 minutes, or until heated through.

Serves 6

Sautéed Yellow Plantains with Parmesan Cheese
(Amarillos con Queso Parmesano)

While looking for healthier ways to cook our staple root vegetables, I came across this simple recipe. It is good with fish or chicken.

2 **tablespoons butter or margarine**
2 **tablespoons light olive oil**
3 **very ripe plantains, peeled and cut into ½-inch slices**
¼ **cup grated Parmesan cheese**

Heat the butter and oil in a nonstick skillet. Sauté the plantain slices over medium heat until golden brown. Drain on paper towels and sprinkle the cheese on top.

Serves 6

Roasted Yellow Plantains with Balsamic Vinegar
(Amarillos con Vinagre Balsámico)

Balsamic vinegar combined with brown sugar gives sweet yellow plantains just the right touch. They go perfectly with a rice-and-bean stew.

- **3 medium ripe plantains**
- **3 tablespoons butter**
- **1 tablespoon balsamic vinegar**
- **1 tablespoon brown sugar**
- **Ground cinnamon for garnish**

Preheat the oven to 400°F. Make a slit in each plantain and place them on a cookie sheet. Bake for 40 minutes. Melt the butter in a saucepan and add the vinegar and sugar to it. Peel the plantains and arrange them on a platter. Drizzle with the butter mixture and garnish with cinnamon.

Serves 6

Traditional Mofongo
(Mofongo Tradicional)

This superb dish combines green plantains with pork cracklings and fresh garlic. It is served with chicken broth. I prefer to use bacon instead of cracklings.

- **3 large green plantains**
- **3 cups water mixed with ½ tablespoon salt**
- **½ pound bacon, diced**
- **3 garlic cloves, peeled and chopped**
- **3 sweet chili peppers, seeded and minced**
- **¼ cup extra virgin olive oil**
-    **Salt and pepper to taste**
- **¼ cup corn oil**

Peel the plantains and cut them into ½-inch slices, dropping them into the salted water. Sauté the bacon and drain and discard the fat. Chop coarsely and set aside. Combine the garlic, chili peppers, and olive oil and season with salt and pepper. Heat the corn oil and fry the plantain slices until golden brown. Drain on paper towels. Put a few teaspoons of the garlic-oil mix in a mortar. Add one-sixth of the bacon and 5 or 6 slices of plantain. Mash and press firmly into the mortar. Invert onto a plate. Repeat the process five more times.

Makes 6 mofongos

New Plantain Dumplings Stuffed with Shrimp
(Nuevo Mofongo Relleno de Camarones)

One of the new trends is mofongo *stuffed with seafood. This recipe was inspired by Tino's Restaurant on the west coast of Puerto Rico.*

STUFFING

- 2 tablespoons extra virgin olive oil
- 3 large garlic cloves, peeled and crushed
- ¼ pound smoked ham, diced
- ¼ cup sliced scallion
- ¼ cup roughly chopped cilantro
- ½ cup chopped manzanilla olives
  Juice of ½ lime
- 1 cup tomato purée
- 1 cup tomato sauce
- 2 pounds medium shrimp, peeled, cleaned, and cut in half

MOFONGO

- 3 large or 6 medium green plantains
- ¼ cup corn oil

Heat the olive oil in a large skillet. Add the remaining stuffing ingredients, except the shrimp, and sauté over medium heat for 5 minutes. Add the shrimp and cook until they turn pink. Set aside.

Peel the plantains and cut them into ½-inch slices. Heat the corn oil in a large skillet and fry the plantain slices until golden brown. Drain on paper towels.

Mash 5 or 6 plantain slices in a mortar with a little of the stuffing liquid. Fold in ½ cup of the shrimp mixture and shape into a ball with your hands. Repeat the process five more times.

Serves 6

Pasteles

Pasteles *are like a rainbow. Cubed pork and smoked ham mixed with raisins,* alcaparrado, *chick-peas, and other ingredients form the traditional stuffing. New stuffings include lobster and shrimp and vegetables like zucchini. (See the stuffing recipes that follow.)*

The dough is an intriguing combination of assorted shredded root vegetables and tubers. Traditionally, this mixture is wrapped in banana or plantain leaves. Parchment paper or aluminum foil can be used if these are unavailable.

Pasteles *can be eaten year-round, but they are an essential Christmas dish on the island and for Puerto Ricans on the mainland.*

1¼ pounds *yautía* (taro root)
3 pounds unripe (green) bananas
¾ pound potatoes
1 green plantain
2 tablespoons milk
¼ cup annatto oil, plus extra to grease the leaves or parchment paper (see page 8)
   Salt to taste
   Banana leaves, plantain leaves, parchment paper, or aluminum foil for wrapping
   Traditional Pork Filling or Lobster Filling (see page 102)
   Salted water to boil *pasteles*

Peel the vegetables and soak them in salted water for 5 minutes. Drain and grate on the finest side of the grater. Add the milk, oil, and salt. Let the dough rest for at least 1 hour in the refrigerator. (It is better if refrigerated overnight.) Brush the leaves or parchment paper with annatto oil. Spread ½ cup of the dough onto the center of an 8 × 10-inch wrapper. Place 2 tablespoons of the filling on the left side of the dough. Fold about 2½ inches from the left side of the wrapper. Fold twice more. Fold 2½ inches from the top and bottom. You should have a rectangle about 3½ inches wide and 6½ inches long. Tie with butcher's twine. Bring the water to a boil in a large soup pot. Add the *pasteles* and bring to a boil again. Reduce the heat and simmer, covered, for 45 minutes, turning the *pasteles* once.

Makes 16 pasteles

TRADITIONAL PORK FILLING

½ pound boneless pork shoulder, cut into small pieces
  Adobo to taste (see page 15)
2 tablespoons annatto oil (see page 8)
4 ounces ham, diced
½ cup Basic *Recaíto* (see page 16)
1 8-ounce can tomato sauce
¼ cup golden raisins
⅓ cup chick-peas
½ cup manzanilla olives
1 6-ounce jar pimientos, drained and chopped
1 teaspoon salt
1 teaspoon black pepper
1 tablespoon dried oregano
  Hot sauce to taste
2 tablespoons shredded unsweetened coconut

Season the pork with *adobo*. Heat the oil in a skillet and sauté the pork and ham for 5 minutes over medium heat. Add the remaining ingredients. Reduce the heat to medium-low and cook for 25 minutes, or until the pork is cooked through. Cool to room temperature before using.

Makes enough stuffing for 16 pasteles

LOBSTER FILLING
  1 tablespoon annatto oil (see page 8) combined with 1
    tablespoon light olive oil
  ¼ cup Basic *Recaíto* (see page 16)
  ¼ cup currants
  ½ cup sliced manzanilla olives
  ½ cup tomato sauce
  1 pound cooked lobster meat, diced
  2 teaspoons salt
  1 teaspoon black pepper

Heat the oil in a heavy skillet until hot but not smoking.
Add the *recaíto,* currants, and olives. Sauté for 2 minutes. Add
the tomato sauce, lobster, and salt and pepper. Cook over medium heat for 5 minutes. Cool to room temperature before using.

Makes enough stuffing for 16 pasteles.

Baked Puerto Rican Yam
(Batata Asada)

Simple yet packed with sweetness and flavor, baked batatas *can be used like baked potatoes.*

6 *batatas* (Puerto Rican yams), scrubbed
6 tablespoons (¾ stick) butter

Preheat the oven to 400°F. Rub 1 tablespoon of the butter on each *batata*. Set the *batatas* in a pan and bake for 1 hour.

Serves 6

Puerto Rican Yam Fries
(Batatas Fritas)

*This traditional side dish for roasted chicken is sold along the roads
on the island. You can also pan-fry the slices.*

> 3 pounds *batatas* (Puerto Rican yams)
>   Salted water for soaking
> 2 cups corn oil
> 1 teaspoon black pepper
>   Ground nutmeg to taste (optional)

Peel the *batatas* and cut them into ¼-inch slices. Soak the
slices in salted water to cover for 15 minutes. Drain and pat
dry. Heat the oil in a skillet and fry the *batata* slices in a single
layer until golden brown on both sides. Drain on paper towels
and sprinkle with pepper and nutmeg to taste.

Serves 6

Cassava Fries in Garlic Oil
(Yuca con Mojo de Ajo)

Yuca *(cassava) with garlic oil is a staple peasant side dish. It is usually eaten with* bacalao *(salt codfish), fried fish, or chicken.*

4   large garlic cloves, peeled and chopped
1   sprig fresh thyme
½   cup sunflower or other vegetable oil
3   pounds *yuca* (cassava)
2   quarts water combined with 1 tablespoon salt
1   cup corn oil

Combine the garlic, thyme, and oil. Set aside. Peel the *yuca* and cut it in "steak fry" 3 × ½ × ½-inch strips. Boil the salted water in a large soup pot, add the *yuca,* and cook for 30 minutes. Do not overcook; the *yuca* should have a firm texture. Drain and pat dry with paper towels. Heat the oil in a heavy skillet. Sauté the *yuca* until golden brown. Drain on paper towels. Arrange the strips on a platter, and pour the garlic oil over the "fries."

Serves 6

Sweet-and-Sour Cassava
(Yuca Agridulce)

A simple and different way to serve yuca *(cassava) as a side dish.*

3 pounds *yuca* (cassava), cut into small dice (about 3
    cups)
   Salted water
2 tablespoons butter
2 tablespoons soy sauce
1½ tablespoons brown sugar

Cook the *yuca* in the salted water for 25 minutes. Drain and
set aside.

Melt the butter in a frying pan. Add the soy sauce and sugar. When butter mixture starts to bubble, add the *yuca*. Sauté
over medium-high heat for 5 minutes.

Serves 6

Cassava Chili
(Chili de Yuca)

Yuca (cassava) and white beans replace beef and red kidney beans in this vegetarian variation of the traditional chili con carne.

3½   pounds *yuca* (cassava), peeled and cubed
       Salted water
  2   tablespoons annatto oil (see page 8) combined with 1 tablespoon corn oil
  ¼   cup Basic *Recaíto* (see page 16)
  1   16-ounce can whole tomatoes, drained, seeded, and chopped
1¼   cups tomato purée
  1   cup tomato sauce
2½   cups white navy beans, cooked
1½   teaspoons chili powder
  2   teaspoons salt
       Pinch ground nutmeg

Boil the *yuca* in the salted water for 25 minutes. Drain and set aside.

Heat the oil in a large skillet and add the *recaíto*, tomatoes, tomato purée, and tomato sauce. Cook the mixture for 5 minutes over medium-low heat. Add the beans, *yuca,* and seasonings. Cook for 10 more minutes.

Serves 6

Pickled Medallions of Taro Root
(*Medallones de Yautía en Escabeche*)

Try serving this as an alternative to yams on Thanksgiving Day!

½ cup white vinegar
1¼ cups plus 3 tablespoons olive oil
½ tablespoon salt
½ tablespoon black pepper
½ cup roughly chopped manzanilla olives
3 bay leaves
1 pound yellow onions, sliced
2½ pounds *yautía* (taro root), peeled

In a bowl, whisk the vinegar and the 1¼ cups olive oil. Add the salt, pepper, olives, and bay leaves. Set aside. Heat the 3 tablespoons olive oil, and sauté the onion slightly. Add the onion to the dressing.

In a large soup pot, cover the *yautía* with cold water and bring to a boil. Reduce the heat and simmer for 20 minutes, or until the *yautía* is tender. Drain and cool completely.

Cut the *yautía* into 1-inch-thick medallions and toss with the dressing.

Serves 4

8

FISH AND SHELLFISH
(Pescados y Mariscos)

Living on an island with the Caribbean Sea on one side and the Atlantic Ocean on the other has allowed us access to a great variety of fish and shellfish. Our typical seafood dishes display our Spanish heritage clearly, as they are mostly prepared in a *sofrito*-based sauce or *escabeche* style. *Bacalao* (salt cod) has been an important staple for centuries. It is cheap, readily available, and keeps without refrigeration.

One of our favorite fish has always been red snapper. Shellfish include shrimp, *langostinos* (saltwater crayfish), mussels, and the spiny lobster characteristic of Caribbean Sea waters. Conch and octopus are used mostly in salads.

The introduction of sophisticated herbs such as tarragon has led to the evolution of delicate sauces to use over fish. Poaching has been incorporated as a cooking method to keep up with trends toward lower fat consumption.

Fish in Mojito Isleño Sauce
(Pescado en Salsa de Mojito Isleño)

This is a classic dish that is served throughout the island's coastal towns. Mojito isleño, a sauce that originated in Salinas, combined with red snapper is delicious evidence that simple cooking can also make a memorable meal.

3 whole red snappers (1 to 1½ pounds each), each split lengthwise into 2 pieces
½ tablespoon *Adobo* (see page 15)
¼ cup corn oil
1 recipe *Mojito Isleño* (see page 21)

Season the fish with the *adobo*. Heat the oil in a large skillet and sauté the fish until golden brown on both sides. Transfer the fish to another pan and add the sauce. Bring to a boil, then reduce the heat and simmer for 15 minutes, or until the fish is cooked through.

Serves 6

Pickled Fish
(*Pescado en Escabeche*)

My friend Miguelina serves this dish as a Lenten specialty. Traditionally sierra, Spanish mackerel, is used, but I prefer to use blue snapper.

1 **lemon, cut in half**
6 **blue snapper steaks, 1 inch thick (about 3 pounds total)**
1 **cup all-purpose flour seasoned with 2 teaspoons each salt and black pepper**
1 **cup corn oil**
1 **recipe *Escabeche* Sauce (see page 17)**

Squeeze the lemon over the fish steaks and dredge them in the seasoned flour. Heat the oil and fry the fish until golden brown on both sides. Drain on paper towels. Set the fish in a nonreactive bowl and pour the *escabeche* sauce over it. Let it marinate for at least 2 hours or overnight.

Serves 6

Swordfish Marinated in Recaíto
(Pez Espada Marinado en Recaíto)

Recaíto, a staple seasoning, highlights a marinade to make swordfish sweet and pungent.

MARINADE

½ cup olive oil
¼ cup tomato sauce
½ cup Basic *Recaíto* (see page 16)
¾ cup fresh orange juice
3 bay leaves

6 swordfish steaks

SAUCE

¼ cup (½ stick) butter
½ cup fresh orange juice
½ cup frozen passion fruit juice concentrate, thawed
2 garlic cloves, peeled and chopped
1 tablespoon Dijon mustard
  Zest of 1 small orange, or more to taste
2 tablespoons olive oil
1 red bell pepper, seeded and diced, for garnish
¼ cup chopped cilantro for garnish

Combine the marinade ingredients in a bowl. Add the fish, cover, and refrigerate for 2 hours. Turn the steaks every hour.

While the fish is marinating, prepare the sauce. Melt the butter and add the remaining ingredients, except the oil, bell pepper, and cilantro, and bring the mixture to a boil. Reduce the heat and simmer until the liquid is reduced to ⅔ cup. Set aside.

Drain the fish and discard the marinade. Heat the oil in a nonstick skillet and sauté the fish until lightly browned on both sides.

To serve, arrange the fish on a platter and pour the sauce over it. Sprinkle the bell pepper and cilantro on top.

Serves 6

Fish Sticks
(Palitos de Pescado)

These fish sticks are excellent party food. Serve with sofrito *dipping sauce.*

>   2 **pounds sea bass, trout, or tile fish fillets**
>   1 **tablespoon** *Adobo* **(see page 15)**
>   3 **cups corn oil**
>   1 **egg, beaten**
>   1½ **cups bread crumbs**
>   1½ **cups all-purpose flour**

Cut the fish in strips 2 inches long and ½ inch wide. Season with the *adobo*. Roll the strips gently to "round" them.

Heat the oil in a frying pan. While the oil is getting hot, dip the fish strips, one at a time, in the egg. Let any excess egg drip off. Dredge each strip in bread crumbs and then in flour. Shake off any excess. Fry the strips in small batches until golden brown.

Serves 4 to 6

NOTE: You can keep the fish sticks warm in a 250°F oven.

Scrambled Eggs with Salt Codfish
(*Bacalao con Huevos Revueltos*)

Bacalao *(salt codfish) has been a staple food for centuries in Puerto Rico. During the Depression years it was called "the steak of the poor." This is the simplest of our daily* bacalao *dishes.*

 3 tablespoons corn oil
 1 medium yellow onion, sliced
 1 red bell pepper, seeded and cut into strips
1½ pounds *bacalao* (salt codfish), cooked and shredded
    (see page 8)
 6 eggs, lightly beaten
 1 teaspoon black pepper, or to taste

Heat the oil in a skillet and sauté the onion and bell pepper over medium heat until the onion just browns. Add the codfish and eggs and cook until the eggs are set. Season with black pepper.

Serves 6

Salt Codfish with Spinach
(Bacalao con Espinacas)

*Fried codfish is one of my father's favorite dishes. I have added
sautéed spinach and prunes for a sweet touch.*

1½ pounds *bacalao* (salt codfish), cooked and drained but
    not shredded (see page 8)
1 cup all-purpose flour
2 teaspoons black pepper
2 cups corn oil
3 tablespoons light olive oil
⅓ cup sliced almonds
10 prunes, pitted and chopped
1 10-ounce package frozen chopped spinach, thawed
    and drained

Combine the flour and pepper on a plate. Cut the codfish
into 2- to 3-inch pieces and coat lightly with the flour.

Heat the corn oil in a skillet and fry the codfish until golden
brown on both sides. Drain on paper towels, set aside, and
keep warm. In another pan, heat the olive oil and sauté the almonds until lightly browned. Add the prunes and spinach and
cook over medium heat for 5 minutes. To serve, divide the codfish on serving plates, then top with the spinach mixture.

Serves 6

Salt Codfish Stew
(Bacalao Guisado)

This stew was served as everyday lunch food for centuries. Freshly harvested boiled root vegetables are the perfect side dish for this genuine peasant delicacy!

2 tablespoons annatto oil (see page 8)
½ cup Basic *Recaíto* (see page 16)
6 plum tomatoes, diced
1 cup tomato sauce
2 pounds *bacalao* (salt codfish), cooked and shredded
   (see page 8)
2 bay leaves
1 teaspoon salt
1 teaspoon black pepper

Heat the oil in a skillet and add the *recaíto*, tomatoes, and tomato sauce. Cook over medium heat for 5 minutes. Add the remaining ingredients and cook over low heat for 15 minutes.

Serves 6

Salt Codfish Salad
(Ensalada de Bacalao)

I spent some time on a farm in Naguabo, located on Puerto Rico's east coast. I remember how Don Sabad would go to the field in the morning and get some yautías (taro roots), plátanos (plantains), and panapén (breadfruit). His wife, Doña Ana, an excellent cook, would put together three stones in the backyard, where a fire would be built. Over this open fire we would prepare a delicious lunch of bacalao (salt codfish) salad and boiled viandas (root vegetables). The yellow bell peppers add a colorful touch to this traditional dish.

1½ pounds *bacalao* (salt codfish), cooked and shredded (see page 8)
1 large potato, boiled, peeled and cut into chunks
1 medium Spanish onion, peeled and minced
1 avocado, peeled and cut into chunks
3 hard-boiled eggs, sliced
1 red and 1 yellow bell pepper, seeded and cut into strips
1 tomato, seeded and chopped
⅓ cup white vinegar
1 cup olive oil
Salt and pepper to taste

In a serving bowl, combine the codfish with the potato, onion, avocado, egg, peppers, and tomato. In a separate bowl, combine the vinegar and oil and season to taste. Pour the dressing over the codfish mixture and toss well.

Serves 4 to 6

Coconut Shrimp
(Camarones con Coco)

This shrimp dish, crispy on the outside yet tender inside, is great party food. It is even better served over a bed of Coquí Rice (see page 163).

   2 **cups coconut milk**
   1 **egg, beaten**
  24 **jumbo shrimp, peeled and cleaned**
  ½ **cup unsweetened shredded coconut**
  ½ **cup sweetened shredded coconut**
   1 **cup all-purpose flour**
   1 **tablespoon baking powder**
   1 **tablespoon *Adobo* (see page 15)**
  ¼ **cup corn oil**

Combine the coconut milk and egg in a large bowl. Add the shrimp and marinate for 30 minutes. Blend the remaining ingredients, except the corn oil, by pulsing a few times in a food processor. Drain the shrimp and discard the marinade. Dredge the shrimp in the coconut-flour mixture. Heat the oil and fry the shrimp until golden brown on both sides. Drain on paper towels.

Serves 12 as an appetizer or 6 as a main dish

Shrimp, Papaya, and Avocado Platter

(Plato de Camarones, Papaya, y Aguacate)

Papayas and avocados are so abundant on the island that they are everyday foods. I created this recipe inspired by the bright colors of these fruits (yes, avocado is a fruit) during my days on Wall Street. It was served for a corporate Christmas lunch. Miriam and Nelson, my co-workers, had a lot of fun preparing it to serve 500 people!

Salted water or chicken stock to boil shrimp
Juice of 1 lemon
1 lemon, cut in half
1 Italian frying pepper (or bell pepper), seeded and diced
½ medium yellow onion, peeled and diced
2 pounds medium shrimp, peeled and cleaned
2 tablespoons brandy (optional)
⅓ cup fruit vinegar (my favorite is raspberry)
1 cup olive oil
¾ cup coarsely chopped cilantro
1 teaspoon salt
½ teaspoon white pepper
2 cups Boston lettuce leaves, cleaned
2 medium avocados
2 papayas

Combine the water, lemon juice, lemon, frying pepper, and onion in a pot large enough to hold the liquid and shrimp. Bring to a boil. Add the shrimp and cook for 5 minutes, or until they turn pink. Drain and cool.

In a bowl, whisk the brandy, vinegar, oil, cilantro, salt, and pepper. Reserve ⅓ cup. Pour the rest over the shrimp and let it marinate in the refrigerator for at least an hour or overnight.

Line a platter with the lettuce. Peel and slice the avocados and papayas and alternate slices of each. Brush with the reserved dressing. Drain the shrimp and put them in the middle of the platter.

Serves 6 to 8

Paella Río Mar

Paella, the national dish of Spain, has become a staple rice dish on the island. Traditional versions include meats, poultry, and seafood.

Accentuated by saffron, this is a simple combination of shellfish and rice. This recipe was inspired by the Río Mar resort located on the east coast of Puerto Rico. At Río Mar the breeze from El Yunque Rain Forest meets the sea, creating a peaceful and pleasant environment.

⅓	cup light olive oil
1	medium yellow onion, peeled and diced
1	yellow bell pepper, seeded and diced
4	garlic cloves, peeled and chopped
3	cups parboiled long-grain rice
4½ to 5	cups boiling chicken stock
	Generous pinch saffron, soaked in an additional 1 cup boiling chicken stock
2	teaspoons salt
½	teaspoon black pepper
12	mussels, in shells, cleaned
12	clams, in shells, cleaned
½	cup water or white wine
1	pound medium shrimp, peeled and cleaned (save shells for broth)
4	lobster tails, shelled and cut into small pieces (save shells for broth)
1	cup frozen tiny green peas, thawed
1	6-ounce jar pimientos, drained and cut into strips

Heat the oil in a paella pan or Dutch oven. Sauté the onion, pepper, and garlic over medium heat for 5 minutes. Stir in the rice and mix well. Add stock to cover, then add the cup with saffron. Add the salt and pepper. Bring the rice to a boil.

In a large pot, steam the clams and mussels in water or

wine; drain and set aside. Add the shrimp, lobster, and peas to the rice and mix well. Reduce the heat and simmer for 20 minutes, or until the rice is cooked. Mix the clams and mussels into the rice just before serving. Transfer the paella to a platter. Garnish with pimiento strips.

Serves 10 to 12

Shrimp Stew
(Camarones a La Criolla)

Salinas, a town located on the south coast of the island, is best known for its seafood restaurants. For many years Ladi's was the most famous of these. Any special occasion would merit a trip to this beautiful part of the island.

I have sweet memories of walking along the beach and eating endless plates of tostones (fried green plantains) while waiting for a dish of succulent shrimp stew served on a bed of white rice with beans on the side.

- 1 tablespoon annatto oil (see page 8) combined with 2 tablespoons olive oil
- ¼ cup Basic *Recaíto* (see page 16)
- 3 bay leaves
- ½ cup *alcaparrado* or manzanilla olives
- 3 ounces smoked ham, cut into small dice
- 1 cup tomato sauce
- 1 16-ounce can whole tomatoes, drained and roughly chopped
- 2 pounds medium shrimp, peeled and cleaned
- 2 teaspoons salt
- 2 teaspoons black pepper

Heat the oil in a soup pot. Add the *recaíto*, bay leaves, *alcaparrado*, and ham. Sauté over medium-high heat for 3 minutes. Add the tomato sauce and canned tomato. Bring the mixture to a boil, reduce the heat to medium, and add the shrimp. Cook until the shrimp turn pink, about 5 minutes. Stir in salt and pepper and cook 2 minutes more.

Serves 6 to 8

Octopus Salad
(*Ensalada de Pulpo*)

The most popular beach on the west coast of Puerto Rico is Boquerón. There are kiosks on the beach that sell all kinds of traditional delicacies. Octopus salad served in a paper cone is a favorite for beachgoers.

Traditional ingredients include white vinegar and yellow onions. Red onions impart color and raspberry vinegar a subtle flavor.

3½ **pounds fresh or precooked octopus**
 4 **bay leaves**
½ **tablespoon black peppercorns**
 2 **sprigs cilantro**
 1 **teaspoon salt**
¼ **cup raspberry vinegar**
¾ **cup olive oil**
½ **cup manzanilla olives**
½ **medium red onion, finely chopped**
   Black pepper to taste

If using fresh octopus, in a large pot combine the octopus, bay leaves, peppercorns, cilantro, and water to cover, and bring to a boil. Reduce the heat and simmer for 1 hour. Drain and cool. Clean the octopus by cutting out the eyes and cut it into small pieces.

Whisk the remaining ingredients in a bowl. Add to the cooked octopus and refrigerate for at least 1 hour before serving, although it's better if left overnight.

Serves 6

9

POULTRY
(Aves)

Poultry recipes, like those for seafood, exhibit our rich Spanish heritage. Chicken is eaten almost every day.

Turkey was once prepared only for the Thanksgiving holiday. Today, on the island as on the mainland, turkey parts are available year-round and are seasoned with ingredients like *adobo*. New dishes include chicken with fruit sauces, roasted chicken stuffed with *mofongo*, and various birds in *escabeche* sauce made with red onions.

Traditional Chicken with Rice
(Arroz con Pollo Tradicional)

On all Spanish Caribbean islands, arroz con pollo *is a classic preparation. It is an easy one-pot dish.*

2 garlic cloves, peeled and chopped
1 tablespoon cider vinegar
1 tablespoon *Adobo* (see page 15)
1 4-pound chicken, cut into pieces (you can also use thighs and legs combined)
⅓ cup corn oil or 2 tablespoons annatto oil (see page 8) combined with 3 tablespoons corn oil
⅓ cup olive oil
1 medium yellow onion, sliced
2 Italian frying peppers, seeded and cut into small dice (or 1 green bell pepper cut into strips)
¼ cup Basic *Recaíto* (see page 16)
1 cup tomato sauce
1 12-ounce can beer
3 cups short-grain rice
3½ cups boiling chicken stock
½ cup *alcaparrado,* or to taste
2 teaspoons dried oregano
2 teaspoons salt
1 teaspoon black pepper
1 cup cooked peas and carrots for garnish

Combine the garlic, vinegar, and *adobo* and season the chicken with the mixture. Let it rest in the refrigerator for 1 hour, or better yet, overnight.

Heat the corn oil in a large skillet and sauté the chicken over medium heat for 5 minutes. Drain and set aside. Heat the olive oil in a large skillet and sauté the onion and pepper until the onion is lightly browned. Add the *recaíto,* tomato sauce, beer, and chicken. Continue cooking over medium-low heat for 5 minutes.

Stir in all the remaining ingredients except the peas and carrots and bring to a boil. Reduce the heat to low, stir well, cover, and cook for 30 minutes or until all the liquid has evaporated. To serve, arrange the rice and chicken on a platter and sprinkle the peas and carrots on top.

Serves 8

Chicken and Rice with Asparagus and Tarragon

(Arroz con Pollo con Espárragos y Estragón)

Traditional arroz con pollo *gets refined by substituting asparagus for green peas and chicken thigh strips for whole chicken pieces. Fresh tarragon, a natural with chicken, replaces cilantro, a staple in many chicken dishes. The bright annatto oil is omitted, giving this island dish a subtle and appetizing color.*

         2 tablespoons corn oil
         2 ounces ham, cut into small dice
         4 chicken thighs, skinned, boned, and cut into
            strips
         1 medium red bell pepper, seeded and sliced
         2 tablespoons fresh tarragon leaves, minced, or
            2 teaspoons dried
         1 cup tomato sauce
        2½ cups long-grain rice
  4 to 4½ cups chicken stock or canned chicken broth
         ½ pound fresh asparagus spears, blanched, for
            garnish

Heat the oil in a large saucepan. Add the ham and chicken and sauté until the chicken is browned, about 5 minutes. Add the bell pepper and sauté for another 2 minutes. Add the tarragon and tomato sauce and bring to a simmer. Add the rice and chicken stock and bring to a boil. Cover, reduce the heat, and simmer until the rice is tender, 20 to 25 minutes. Garnish with the asparagus and serve.

Serves 6

Chicken with Rice Aibonito
(Arroz con Pollo a lo Aibonito)

Aibonito, hometown of Dennis Rivera (president of Local 1199, New York City's hospital workers' union), produces the best chickens on the island. This small town also has an annual flower show. Inspired by the many colors of the fresh flowers, I created this dish. It is a variation of the classic arroz con pollo.

2 **whole bone-in chicken breasts with skin, cut into 2-inch pieces**
1 **recipe Traditional Garlic Dipping Sauce (see page 20)**
¼ **cup olive oil**
½ **cup black olives, pitted and chopped**
⅓ **cup golden raisins**
½ **cup green peas**
1 **6-ounce jar pimientos, drained and cut in strips**
4 **cups long-grain rice**
4 to 5 **cups chicken stock**
Generous pinch saffron, soaked in an additional 1 cup boiling chicken stock
2 **teaspoons salt**
1 **teaspoon black pepper**

Marinate the chicken pieces in the dipping sauce for 30 minutes. Drain and discard the liquid. In a skillet, heat 2 teaspoons oil, lightly sauté the chicken pieces, and set aside. Heat the remaining olive oil in a Dutch oven. Sauté the olives, raisins, peas, and pimientos for 5 minutes. Stir in the rice. Add enough chicken stock, including the cup with saffron, to cover the rice, and bring to a boil. Add salt and pepper. Reduce the heat and add the chicken. Simmer for 20 minutes, or until the rice and chicken are cooked.

Serves 10 to 12

Chicken with Macaroni
(Macarrones con Pollo)

This is a dish with an Italian influence, but the sofrito *definitely gives it a Puerto Rican touch.*

½ **pound rigatoni, cooked according to package instructions**
2 **tablespoons annatto oil (see page 8)**
¼ **pound smoked ham, diced**
¼ **cup Basic *Recaíto* (see page 16)**
2 **pounds chicken pieces, seasoned with *Adobo* (see page 15)**
¼ **cup manzanilla olives, chopped**
1 **tablespoon capers**
1 **cup tomato sauce**
½ **teaspoon black pepper**
½ **cup grated Parmesan cheese**

Put the cooked pasta in a bowl. Heat the oil in a skillet and sauté the ham and *recaíto* over medium heat for 3 minutes. Add the chicken, olives, and capers and cook for 5 minutes. Add the tomato sauce and bring to a boil. Reduce the heat to medium-low and cook, covered, for 20 minutes. Add the pasta, pepper, and cheese and toss well.

Serves 6

Traditional Chicken Fricassee
(*Fricasé de Pollo Tradicional*)

Traditionally, this chicken stew dish was made with red wine. I prefer to use golden rum for a lighter touch.

1 **4-pound chicken, cut into pieces**
1 **tablespoon salt**
1 **teaspoon black pepper**
½ **tablespoon dried oregano**
3 **tablespoons safflower oil**
4 **ounces smoked ham, diced**
½ **cup Basic *Recaíto* (see page 16)**
1 **Italian frying pepper, seeded and diced**
½ **cup *alcaparrado***
1 **tablespoon white-wine vinegar**
2 **cups tomato sauce**
2 **cups water**
½ **cup golden rum**
3 **bay leaves**

Season the chicken with salt, pepper, and oregano. Set aside. Heat the oil in a large skillet and sauté the ham, *recaíto*, frying pepper, and *alcaparrado* over medium heat for 5 minutes. Add the chicken and cook for 5 minutes more. Stir in the remaining ingredients. Bring to a boil, then reduce the heat and simmer for 25 minutes.

Serves 6

Chicken Stew with Cinnamon
(Pollo Guisado con Canela)

This was a specialty of my husband's grandmother. Serve it on a bed of white rice.

1 3- to 3½-pound chicken, cut into pieces
   Adobo to taste (see page 15)
3 tablespoons annatto oil (see page 8)
½ cup Basic *Recaíto* (see page 16)
8 ounces smoked ham, diced
1 cup tomato sauce
1 16-ounce can whole tomatoes, cut into pieces
1 cup water
½ tablespoon ground cinnamon
1 teaspoon salt
1 teaspoon black pepper

Season the chicken with the *adobo*. Refrigerate for 30 minutes. Heat the oil in a skillet and sauté the *recaíto* and ham over medium heat for 5 minutes. Add the tomato sauce, tomatoes, and water and bring to a boil. Add the chicken, cinnamon, salt, and pepper, and bring to a boil again. Reduce the heat to low and simmer for 30 minutes.

Serves 6

Pickled Chicken
(Pollo en Escabeche)

Red onions make this everyday dish a festive one!

3 **pounds chicken pieces**
   Adobo **to taste (see page 15)**
3 **tablespoons corn oil**
1 **recipe** *Escabeche* **Sauce using red onions (see page 17)**

Season the chicken with the *adobo*. Heat the oil in a large skillet and sauté the chicken until it is lightly browned. Remove from the pan and drain on paper towels.

Bring the *escabeche* sauce to a boil in a Dutch oven. Lower the heat, add the chicken pieces, and simmer for 35 minutes, or until the chicken is tender.

Serves 6

Ginger-Citrus Chicken
(Pollo en Salsa de Gengibre y Frutas Cítricas)

Ginger is not commonly used for savory dishes on the island. Here, combined with citrus fruits, it makes a spectacular sauce for chicken.

6 **chicken thighs, boned and skinned**
4 **teaspoons salt**
2 **teaspoons black pepper**
   Juice of 2 large oranges
3 **tablespoons butter**
1 **2-inch piece fresh ginger, peeled and cut into strips**
1 **orange, peeled and sectioned**
   Juice of 1 lemon

Season the chicken with the salt and pepper and marinate in ½ cup of the orange juice for 10 minutes. Drain and set aside. Heat the butter in a large skillet and sauté the ginger over medium-high heat until lightly browned. Add the chicken and cook until lightly browned on both sides. Add the orange sections, the remaining orange juice, and the lemon juice. Simmer for 10 more minutes.

Serves 6

Chicken in Citrus Escabeche Sauce
(Pollo en Escabeche de Frutas Cítricas)

Citrus fruits, brought to the New World by the Spanish settlers, are abundant throughout the island.

Inspired by traditional escabeche-style dishes, I combined the fresh juice of my three favorite citrus fruits: oranges, lemons, and limes. The red onion and yellow pepper give the dish a colorful touch.

2 **pounds boneless chicken breast, cut into pieces and lightly flattened with a meat mallet**
    Adobo **to taste (see page 15)**
¾ **cup olive oil**
1 **medium red onion, sliced**
1 **yellow bell pepper, seeded and cut into strips**
3 **garlic cloves, peeled and chopped**
    Juice of 2 oranges, 2 limes, and 2 lemons
3 **tablespoons honey**
3 **tablespoons capers for garnish**

Season the chicken with the *adobo.* Heat ¼ cup of the oil in a large skillet and sauté the chicken over medium-high heat until lightly browned. Let it cool to room temperature on a serving platter. In another pan, heat ¼ cup of the oil and sauté the onion, pepper, and garlic until soft. Add the onion mixture to the chicken. Combine the juices, remaining ¼ cup oil, and honey. Pour over the chicken and toss. Garnish with capers.

Serves 6 to 8

Chicken with Papaya
(Pollo con Papaya)

Chicken and papaya is a dish representative of the island's new cuisine. Pieces of boneless chicken breasts are marinated in papaya juice. It is as perfect a combination as all-American ham and pineapple.

        3 **whole chicken breasts, skinned, boned, and split in half**
        2 **teaspoons salt**
        2 **teaspoons black pepper**
        1 **tablespoon chopped fresh basil**
        2 **cups papaya juice**
    1¼ **cups light olive oil**
        1 **fresh ripe papaya, peeled and cut into slices, for garnish**

Season the chicken with the salt and pepper. Mix the basil and the juice with 1 cup of the oil and pour it over the chicken. Marinate for at least 1 hour.

Drain the meat and discard the marinade. Heat the remaining oil in a skillet over medium-high heat. Quickly sear the chicken on both sides. Lower the heat and cook, partially covered, for 15 minutes, turning the meat once.

To serve, arrange the chicken on a platter and garnish with fresh papaya slices.

Serves 6

Roasted Chicken with Honey-Rum Glaze

(Pollo Asado con Glaceado de Ron y Miel de Abejas)

Honey and rum make the perfect glaze for this simple roasted chicken dish. Serve over rice with green pigeon peas.

1 3- to 3½-pound chicken
    Adobo **to taste (see page 15)**
2 tablespoons golden rum or Spiced Rum (see page 226)
¼ cup honey

Preheat the oven to 400°F. Season the chicken with the *adobo* and set aside. Combine the rum and honey and brush the chicken with a light coat of the glaze. Sprinkle more *adobo* over the chicken. Place the chicken in a roasting pan and cover with aluminum foil.

Bake for 20 minutes. Remove the foil and brush the chicken again with the glaze. Bake, uncovered, for 30 minutes more, brushing the chicken with glaze every 10 minutes. Let the chicken cool a little before carving.

Serves 6

Roasted Chicken Stuffed with Mofongo

(Pollo Asado Relleno con Mofongo)

Mofongo *is an innovative stuffing for chicken. You can also prepare your Thanksgiving turkey with* mofongo *stuffing.*

1 whole 3- to 3½-pound chicken
2 tablespoons *Adobo* (see page 15)
2 tablespoons corn oil
1 recipe Traditional *Mofongo* (see page 99)
½ cup chicken broth

Preheat the oven to 350°F. Season the chicken with the *adobo* and brush with oil. Combine the chicken broth with the *mofongo* and mix until it is moist. (Add more stock if needed.) Stuff the chicken and loosely sew up the opening.

Bake for about 1½ hours, or until the meat is very tender.

Serves 6

142

Cornish Hens in Tamarind Sauce
(Gallinitas en Salsa de Tamarindo)

Tamarind combined with garlic and mushrooms creates a spectacular sauce for roasted Cornish hens.

3 **Cornish hens, seasoned with *Adobo* (see page 15)**
2 **tablespoons light olive oil**
4 **garlic cloves, peeled and chopped**
1 **cup sliced fresh mushrooms**
1 **cup tamarind pulp (see page 12)**
1 **cup chicken stock**
2 **tablespoons sugar**
1 **tablespoon cornstarch**
3 **tablespoons each chopped cilantro and scallion for garnish**

Preheat the oven to 350°F. Bake the Cornish hens for 30 minutes, or until the juices run clear when the breast is pricked with a fork. While the hens are baking, heat the oil in a skillet and sauté the garlic and mushrooms for 5 minutes over medium heat. Set aside. In a blender or food processor, combine the tamarind pulp, chicken stock, and sugar. Set ½ cup of the liquid aside and dissolve the cornstarch in it. Bring the remaining liquid to a boil. Remove the pan from the heat and mix a small amount with the reserved cornstarch mixture. Pour all liquid back into the pan, put the pan back on the stove, and cook over medium-low heat until the sauce is thick enough to coat the back of a spoon. Add the mushrooms and set aside.

When the hens are done, cut each in half and pour sauce over it. Garnish with cilantro and scallion.

Serves 6

10

BEEF AND PORK
(Carne de Res y Cerdo)

Traditionally, our diet has been rich in beef and pork. Roast suckling pig, a national dish, has always been a holiday preparation. Steak and onions is an everyday dish. Roast pork shoulder has become a favorite holiday dish for Puerto Ricans on the mainland who do not have access to a whole pig.

Stuffed pot roast is another favorite dish. Pork ribs are stewed or prepared with yellow rice and green pigeon peas.

Puerto Rican Steak and Onions
(Bistec Encebollado)

This is the traditional steak-and-onions dish. I remember, when I was growing up in Cayey, how my mother used to season the meat and let it marinate for a few days in the refrigerator. She used alcaparrado. *I prefer to use manzanilla olives.*

    2 pounds beef top round, cut into thin slices
    ½ tablespoon salt
       Black pepper to taste
    ⅓ cup white vinegar
    1 cup olive oil
    ½ cup manzanilla olives, sliced
    3 cloves garlic, peeled and chopped
    1 cup green bell pepper strips
    2 cups Spanish yellow onion slices

Pound the meat to tenderize it. Season with salt and pepper. Combine the vinegar and ¾ cup of the olive oil. Add the olives and garlic; set aside. In a nonstick skillet, heat the remaining ¼ cup of oil and sauté the pepper and onion lightly. Remove the pepper and onion with a slotted spoon and set aside.

Reheat the oil remaining in the skillet until very hot and sear the beef on all sides. Return the pepper and onion to the skillet with the meat. Pour the oil-and-vinegar mixture over the meat. Cook over medium to low heat, partially covered, for 20 minutes, or until the meat is tender.

Serves 6

Traditional Corned Beef
(Carne Bif Tradicional)

This is one of my father's favorite dishes.

> 2 yellow plantains
> 1 cup corn oil
> 1 tablespoon olive oil
> ¼ cup Basic *Recaíto* (see page 16)
> ½ cup *alcaparrado*
> 1½ cups tomato sauce
> ¾ cup water or beef stock
> 2 12-ounce cans corned beef
> Black pepper to taste

Peel the plantains and cut them into ½-inch slices. Heat the corn oil in a large skillet and fry until golden brown. Drain on paper towels and set aside.

Heat the olive oil in a separate skillet. Add the *recaíto*, *alcaparrado*, tomato sauce, and water or stock. Cook over medium heat for 5 minutes. Add the corned beef and black pepper. Cook over medium to low heat for 10 minutes. Add the plantain slices and cook for 5 minutes more.

Serves 6

NOTE: You can keep the plantain warm in a low oven. French fries, corn, or mixed vegetables can be substituted for fried plantains. For a more elegant dish, substitute 2 cups blanched broccoli florets and ¼ cup sliced almonds for the fried plantains.

Puerto Rican Pot Roast
(Carne Mechada al Estilo Puertorriqueño)

Pot roast is a dish enjoyed throughout Latin America. Our version is stuffed with smoked ham, olives, and chorizo. *I have added currants for a sweet touch.*

⅓ cup olive oil
3 tablespoons white-wine vinegar
1 tablespoon *Adobo* (see page 15)
½ tablespoon dried oregano
3 to 3½ pounds eye of round

STUFFING

⅓ cup dried currants, soaked in ⅓ cup sherry
½ cup manzanilla olives, chopped
¼ pound smoked ham, diced
1 *chorizo* (red Spanish sausage), chopped

BRAISING MIXTURE

2 cups tomato sauce
2 cups beef broth
⅓ cup sherry from the marinated currants
⅓ cup Basic *Recaíto* (see page 16)
Remaining stuffing

6 red potatoes, cut into pieces

Combine the olive oil, vinegar, *adobo,* and oregano. Season the meat with this mixture. With a sharp knife, cut a large incision through the center of the meat.

Combine all of the stuffing ingredients. Stuff the meat, cover, and let stand for 1 hour.

Sear the meat on all sides in a large pot or Dutch oven over medium-high heat. Combine all of the braising ingredients. Add to the meat and bring to a boil.

Reduce the heat to a simmer and cook for 1 hour. Slice the meat; return it to the liquid. Add the potatoes and cook for 10 minutes, or until the potatoes are done.

Serves 8 to 10

Puerto Rican Roasted Suckling Pig
(Lechón Asado Puertorriqueño)

Our national dish, roast suckling pig, is a festive presentation. Farmers usually pick one that has been specially fed to be prepared on Christmas Day.

These pigs can weigh from 75 to 100 pounds! At home the size of the pig will probably be determined by the size of your oven and the number of people you plan to feed. A 10- to 15-pound baby pig will feed a crowd of 15 to 20 people. Season the meat a few hours before cooking; keep it in the refrigerator overnight if you can.

- ½ cup garlic cloves or to taste, peeled and chopped
- ½ cup coarsely chopped onion
- ½ cup salt
  Black pepper to taste
- 3 tablespoons dried oregano
- 1 cup corn oil
- 1 10- to 15-pound suckling pig, cleaned and ready to cook
  Extra corn oil for basting
- 1 orange (optional)

Preheat the oven to 350°F. Combine the garlic, onion, salt, pepper, and oregano with the oil. Wash and dry the pig thoroughly. Marinate it in the garlic-and-oil mixture for a few hours or overnight.

Set the pig in a large roasting pan. Insert a ball made of aluminum foil into the pig's mouth. Fold the hind legs under the belly and tie them in place. Cover the ears with small pieces of foil. Bake for 3 to 3½ hours, basting occasionally with corn oil, until the leg juices run clear when pricked with a fork.

To serve, transfer the pig to a serving tray and insert the orange into its mouth. Let the pig rest for 10 to 20 minutes before you carve the meat.

Serves 12 to 15

Roasted Baby Suckling Pig with Guava Glaze

(Lechón Asado con Glaceado de Guayaba)

My father had a friend, Bonilla, whose roasted pig was well known in town. People on their way to Ponce would stop at his shop and buy lechón asado con guineitos (roast pork and boiled green bananas).

I have adapted the recipe by using a more manageable-size pig for the home cook. (Traditionally, a 40- to 50-pound pig is used.) When you go to the island you can see men turning pigs over an open fire in the countryside. The guava glaze gives an interesting touch.

1 **10- to 12-pound baby pig, cleaned and ready to cook**
   Adobo **to taste (see page 15)**
2 **lemons, cut in half**
6 **garlic cloves, peeled and crushed**
1 **bunch cilantro, cleaned and chopped**
¼ **cup spicy brown mustard**
¾ **cup guava jelly or preserves**
1 **orange**

Wash and dry the pig. Season it to taste with the *adobo.* Squeeze lemon all over the meat. Combine the garlic and cilantro, and rub the mixture over the pig. Let the pig marinate for several hours.

Preheat the oven to 350°F. Fold the hind legs underneath the belly and tie them in place. Place the pig in a large roasting pan. Combine the mustard with the jelly in a blender or food processor. Brush the entire surface of the pig with the glaze. Roast for 3 to 3½ hours, basting with the remaining glaze several times until the leg juices run clear when pricked with a fork.

To serve, transfer the pig to a serving tray and insert the orange into its mouth. Let the pig rest for 10 to 20 minutes before you carve the meat.

Serves 12 to 15

Roasted Pork Shoulder
(Pernil de Cerdo al Horno)

Puerto Ricans on the mainland have adapted the traditional roast pig to a pork shoulder for convenience and availability.

This recipe is a specialty of La Familia Restaurant in Jersey City, New Jersey.

    8 garlic cloves
    8 black peppercorns (or assorted peppercorns)
    2 teaspoons dried oregano
    2 tablespoons corn oil
    2 tablespoons cider vinegar
    2 tablespoons salt
    1 5½- to 6-pound pork shoulder

Combine the first 6 ingredients in a mortar and crush. Rub the meat well with this "adobo." Let the meat rest for at least 3 hours in the refrigerator, or overnight if possible.

Preheat the oven to 350°F. Bake the pork shoulder in a roasting pan for 3 to 3½ hours, or until the skin is very crispy, turning it every hour.

Serves 6 to 8

Epi's Pork Pot Roast
(Pernil al Caldero al Estilo de Epi)

I spent a summer in New York's South Bronx, where the largest group of Puerto Ricans in the United States lives. There I met Epi, a wonderful home cook who became a dear friend. She showed me a different way of preparing the traditional pork shoulder. The recipe is especially good for the hot summer months when you don't want to use the oven.

1 **4-pound pork shoulder or butt**
1 **tablespoon salt**
1 **tablespoon black pepper**
2 **tablespoons dried oregano**
4 **large garlic cloves, peeled**
⅓ **cup corn oil**
2 to 3 **cups water or chicken stock**

Remove any excess fat and skin from the meat. Make small cuts all over. Wash and dry. In a mortar, combine the salt, pepper, oregano, garlic, and oil. Crush all of the ingredients to make a paste. Rub the meat with this mixture. Place it in a bowl and cover it with plastic wrap. Refrigerate for 2 hours.

In a large pot, brown the meat over high heat. Lower the heat and add the water or stock. Cook, covered, over medium-low heat for 3 hours. Add more liquid if necessary. The pot roast is done when the meat shreds easily. To serve, cut the meat off the bone.

Serves 6

Pork Loin in Tamarind Sauce
(Pernil de Cerdo en Salsa de Tamarindo)

Here pork gets a twist from the savory tamarind sauce. If fresh tamarind is unavailable, frozen pulp can be used.

1 cup tamarind pulp (from 10 shelled tamarind pods), or
  1 cup frozen tamarind pulp, thawed (see page 12)
2 cups beef stock or canned broth
3 tablespoons sugar
1 3- to 3½-pound boneless pork loin, tied crosswise at
  1-inch intervals
2 tablespoons corn oil
1 teaspoon dried oregano
½ tablespoon salt
½ tablespoon black pepper

Combine the tamarind pulp, stock, and sugar in a nonreactive saucepan. Bring to a boil, reduce the heat, and simmer for 5 minutes. Strain the sauce through a colander; discard the solids. Set aside.

Preheat the oven to 350°F. Rub the pork with oil, oregano, salt, and pepper. Transfer the meat to a roasting pan. Roast for 1½ hours, or until a meat thermometer inserted reads 150°F. Transfer to a carving board and let stand for 10 minutes. To serve, warm the sauce over medium heat. Remove and discard the string from the pork. Carve the meat into ¼-inch slices. Transfer a portion of the pork onto each dinner plate and spoon some sauce on top.

Serves 6 to 8

Pork and Eggplant Stew
(Carne de Cerdo Guisada con Berenjena)

Pork is enhanced by eggplant, a meaty-tasting vegetable.

- 2 tablespoons olive oil
- 2½ pounds boneless pork roast, diced
- ½ cup Basic *Recaíto* (see page 16)
- 1 cup tomato sauce
- 2 to 2½ cups water or beef stock
- 2 bay leaves
- 1 teaspoon salt
- ½ teaspoon black pepper
- 1 1-pound eggplant, peeled and diced

Heat the olive oil in a large skillet. Brown the pork. Add the *recaíto*, tomato sauce, liquid, and bay leaves, and bring to a boil. Reduce the heat to a simmer and cook, covered, for 40 minutes. Add the salt, pepper, and eggplant. Continue cooking, covered, for another 20 minutes.

Serves 6

Mom's Fried Pork Chops
(Chuletas Fritas al Estilo de Mami)

This is a traditional everyday main dish on the island. Mami likes to sprinkle the pork chops with white vinegar. Puerto Ricans usually serve them with white rice and bean stew. They can also be served with tostones *and a mixed green salad.*

8 garlic cloves, peeled
1 tablespoon *Adobo* (see page 15)
½ cup olive oil
   White vinegar to taste
6 center-cut pork chops
3 cups corn oil

In a mortar, crush the garlic. Add the *adobo*, olive oil, and vinegar. Use the mixture to season the pork chops. Heat the oil in a skillet. Drain any excess olive-oil mixture from the pork chops. Fry until golden brown.

Serves 6

NOTE: You can season the pork chops and let them marinate in the refrigerator overnight.

Pork Ribs Glazed with *Sofrito*
(Costillas de Cerdo Glaceadas con Sofrito)

Sofrito makes a delicious marinade. Serve these ribs with rice and beans or tostones.

SOFRITO MARINADE
1 tablespoon annatto oil (see page 8)
1 tablespoon olive oil
2 tablespoons cider vinegar
½ cup Basic *Recaíto* (see page 16)
2 cups tomato sauce
2 tablespoons tomato paste
1 teaspoon black pepper
1 tablespoon guava jelly
¼ cup coffee liqueur (such as Kahlúa or Tía Maria)

8 pounds pork ribs (preferably baby back)
Additional coffee liqueur for basting

Heat the oils in a large skillet. Add the vinegar and sauté the *recaíto* over medium heat for 2 minutes. Add the remaining marinade ingredients and cook for 5 more minutes over medium to low heat. Cool the sauce completely.

In a bowl, combine the ribs with the marinade and let sit for at least 1 hour, or overnight.

Preheat the oven to 350°F. Drain the ribs and discard the marinade. Place the meat in a baking pan and bake for 40 minutes. Turn and bake for another 40 minutes, basting with the coffee liqueur every 15 minutes.

Serves 6

RICE, BEANS, AND PASTA
(Arroz, Habichuelas, y Pasta)

In Puerto Rico, rice and beans have been the base of our diet for more than 300 years. Today, Puerto Ricans of all socioeconomic levels still enjoy rice and bean dishes. If there is a dish that identifies us as Puerto Ricans, it is rice and beans.

Rice

Traditionally, rice is eaten twice daily. It is made into dishes that range from appetizers to desserts. Rice flour is used as a breakfast cereal, to make fritters, and in some desserts.

Most of the short-grain white rice we eat is grown in California and processed on the island. In recent years farmers have started to grow rice on Puerto Rican soil, but only on a small scale.

People who came to live on the mainland have adapted traditional dishes to long-grain rice. Most yellow-rice dishes are made with *sofrito*, annatto oil, smoked ham, and *alcaparrado*. (Annatto oil gives the rice its bright and distinctive yellow color.) Brown rice is eaten mostly by vegetarians. Wild rice has become popular as part of the island's new cuisine.

The most distinctive characteristic of Puerto Rican rice dishes is the *pegao,* the crusty bottom of the rice that sticks to the *caldero,* the heavy iron pot rice is cooked in. (A Dutch oven also works well.) *Pegao* is formed by the way we cook the rice. Oil is heated and the rice is quickly sautéed before boiling water is added. Once the liquid is absorbed, the rice is stirred and covered. The rice is stirred several times as it cooks over low heat, and the *pegao* is formed.

Beans

On some parts of the island, beans are also known as *granos.* With the exception of chick-peas, our beans are all native to the New World, are harvested locally, and are usually eaten fresh. We also use dried and canned beans. *Gandules* (green pigeon peas) are our national bean, the only ones we also use frozen. Pink beans are favorites for daily meals. Other beans commonly used are lima, small white, chick-peas, and small red. Pinto and black beans have become part of our repertoire thanks to the growing number of Cuban and Dominican immigrants who have come to live on the island.

In New York I have come across new varieties of beans known as "boutique" beans. They can be used to prepare interesting versions of traditional Puerto Rican dishes. The Christmas lima, calypso, appaloosa, or Jacob's cattle can turn a peasant bean dish into an elegant presentation.

Beans are used mostly in stews and soups. Traditionally, beans were cooked with a piece of smoked ham, *recaíto,* and bay leaves. Many people like to prepare bean stews using the water in which the beans were cooked.

Dried beans are usually soaked overnight and prepared the following day. The cooking chart (see page 172) is based on beans that have been soaked.

All beans start cooking in cold water. Use 3 parts water to 1 part beans. Bring to a boil, then simmer for the recommended time. I grew up adding salt to the beans at the beginning of the cooking process, but after doing extensive research, I learned that beans should be cooked plain and seasoned when they are almost done. This keeps them from toughening. Some foam will form on the surface as beans cook. Remove it as it rises.

Pasta

Most of our Italian-influenced dishes include a combination of pasta, meat, and a tomato-based sauce prepared with *recaíto*. Smoked ham and *chorizo* are also often added. Beef *picadillo* is used to prepare spaghetti, lasagna, and cannelloni; stewed chicken pieces combined with rigatoni are a daily staple. This dish is a specialty at La Taza de Oro restaurant in New York.

Until recently only dry pasta was available. Now fresh pasta shops have opened throughout the San Juan metropolitan area. We can have fresh pasta every day if we want to.

Basic Puerto Rican White Rice
(Arroz Blanco Puertorriqueño Básico)

The crunchy bottom of the rice pan served with bean stew is the best part of the meal!

>   3 tablespoons corn oil
>   2½ cups short-grain rice
> 4 to 4½ cups boiling water

Heat the oil in a medium saucepan with a tight-fitting lid. Add the rice and sauté quickly over medium-high heat for 2 minutes. Add the water and cook until almost all of the liquid has evaporated.

Stir well, reduce the heat to very low, and cover the rice. Cook for 20 more minutes, stirring after 10 minutes.

Serves 6

NOTE: Make sure you scrape the bottom of the pot!

Coquí Rice
(Arroz Coquí)

My friend John Haney and I created this tasty and visually exciting rice dish for his final project at the French Culinary Institute in New York. Coquí is a native rain-forest frog that hops on the bright green grass.

    2 tablespoons corn oil
    4 cups water or chicken stock
    1 teaspoon salt
 2½ cups parboiled long-grain rice
    2 tablespoons butter
  ½ cup shredded carrot
  ½ cup chopped cilantro
  ¼ cup golden raisins (optional)

Bring the oil, water, and salt to a boil in a saucepan with a tight-fitting lid. Add the rice and reduce the heat to a simmer. Cook until the liquid evaporates. Turn the heat to low and cook, covered, for another 10 minutes. Stir the rice to make it fluffy.

Melt the butter in a saucepan. Add the rice, carrot, and cilantro. Cook over medium heat until the carrot and cilantro are slightly wilted. Add the raisins, if desired. Toss the mixture with the rice.

Serves 6

Rice with Coconut
(Arroz con Coco)

A savory coconut rice dish; serve it with Ginger-Citrus Chicken (see page 138).

2½ tablespoons corn oil
 2 cups parboiled long-grain rice
 ¼ cup raisins (optional)
 ¼ cup shredded coconut (preferably unsweetened)
 5 cups boiling water or chicken stock
 2 teaspoons salt
 1 teaspoon white pepper

Heat the oil in a saucepan with a tight-fitting lid. Add the rice, raisins, if desired, and coconut. Sauté lightly. Add the boiling liquid, salt, and pepper. Cook on high heat until the liquid is absorbed. Reduce the heat to very low and cook, covered, stirring every 10 minutes, for 25 minutes.

Serves 6

Rice with Vienna Sausages
(*Arroz con Salchichas*)

This is a typical fonda *dish. Served with bean stew,* tostones, *and a salad, it makes a hearty meal.*

> 1 **9-ounce can Vienna sausages, drained and cut into pieces**
> 1 **tablespoon annatto oil**
> 2 **tablespoons corn oil**
> 2 **tablespoons Basic** *Recaíto* **(see page 16)**
> 1 **cup tomato sauce**
> ½ **cup manzanilla olives, chopped**
> 2 **cups short-grain rice**
> 4 to 4½ **cups boiling water or chicken stock**
> **Salt and pepper to taste**

Combine the sausages, oil, and *recaíto* in a large pot. Sauté quickly over medium-high heat; reduce the heat and add the tomato sauce and the olives. Cook for 5 minutes.

Add the rice and the water and season to taste. Turn the heat back to medium-high and cook until the water is absorbed. Stir the rice well, reduce the heat to low, and cover the pot. Cook for another 20 to 25 minutes.

Serves 4

Rice with Squid
(Arroz con Calamares)

This is the only combined rice dish in our cuisine that is not yellow!

1 tablespoon olive oil
2 6-ounce cans *calamares en su tinta* (cuttlefish in its ink)
½ cup *alcaparrado*
2½ cups short-grain rice
4½ to 5 cups boiling water or chicken stock
2 teaspoons salt
1 teaspoon black pepper

Heat the oil in a saucepan with a tight-fitting lid and sauté the *calamares* over medium heat for 5 minutes. Add the remaining ingredients. Bring the liquid to a boil. Reduce the heat to a simmer and cook until the liquid has evaporated.

Stir the rice, cover, and cook over very low heat for 30 minutes, stirring every 10 minutes.

Serves 6

Basic Yellow Rice
(Arroz Amarillo Básico)

The bright yellow color of this rice reminds me of a beautiful sunny day on the island. This is an everyday rice dish.

> **2 tablespoons annatto oil combined with 1 tablespoon corn oil**
> **2½ cups rice**
> **4 to 4½ cups boiling water or chicken stock**
> **2 teaspoons salt**

Heat the oil in a saucepan with a tight-fitting lid. Add the rice and stir to combine. Stir in the boiling liquid and salt. Bring to a boil, reduce the heat to a simmer, and cook until the liquid evaporates. Cover and cook over very low heat for 20 minutes, stirring after 10 minutes.

Serves 6.

Puerto Rican Fried Rice
(*Arroz Frito al Estilo Puertorriqueño*)

When I was growing up, the Chinese restaurants in my hometown, Cayey, used to serve fried rice made with iceberg lettuce. I have added annatto oil to make it more like our yellow rice dishes.

      4 tablespoons annatto oil (see page 8)
     ¼ cup chopped scallion
     ½ cup chopped Italian frying pepper
      1 cup bean sprouts
     ¼ cup shredded iceberg lettuce
      2 eggs, beaten
    2½ cups cooked rice
     ½ teaspoon salt
     ½ teaspoon black pepper

Heat 2 tablespoons of the annatto oil in a large skillet. Sauté the scallion, Italian pepper, bean sprouts, and lettuce over medium-high heat for 2 minutes. Add the eggs and cook until scrambled soft. Set aside.

In another pan, heat the remaining annatto oil. Add the rice and cook over high heat, stirring constantly, until the rice has become completely yellow. Add the egg mixture, salt, and pepper, turn the heat to medium, and cook for another 2 minutes.

Serves 6

Yellow Rice with Shrimp and Mixed Vegetables

(*Arroz Amarillo con Camarones y Vegetales Mixtos*)

Elsa Ayala from the Commonwealth of Puerto Rico office in New York has a relative of Pakistani background. She has developed what she calls "Paquirican" cuisine. This delicious shrimp with yellow rice is one of her favorite holiday dishes.

- 2 tablespoons annatto oil (see page 8)
- 1 tablespoon corn oil
- 1 pound medium shrimp, peeled and cleaned
- 1 cup frozen mixed vegetables, thawed
- 2½ cups short-grain rice
- 4 cups boiling water or chicken stock
- 2 teaspoons salt
- ½ teaspoon black pepper
- ½ teaspoon curry powder

Heat the oils in a large pot with a tight-fitting lid. Sauté the shrimp over medium-high heat for 2 minutes. Add the mixed vegetables and rice. Toss well and continue cooking for 1 more minute. Add the boiling liquid and seasonings. Cook until the water has evaporated. Stir, lower the heat, and cook for 20 more minutes, stirring after 10 minutes.

Serves 8 to 10

NOTE: If you want rice with a spicier touch, increase the amount of curry powder.

Yellow Rice with Crab
(Arroz con Jueyes)

I originally prepared this rice using crabs I had just caught on a fishing trip with my friend Pablo Baez. If fresh crabs are unavailable, use lump crabmeat. It works just fine.

> 4 tablespoons annatto oil (see page 8)
> 12 crabs, cooked, or 1 pound lump crabmeat
> ½ cup Basic *Recaíto* (see page 16)
> ½ cup manzanilla olives, chopped
> 1 cup tomato sauce
> 3 cups parboiled long-grain rice
> 4 to 4½ cups boiling water (you can use the same water used to cook the crabs)

Heat the oil in a large pot with a tight-fitting lid. Add the crabs or crabmeat, *recaíto*, olives, and tomato sauce. Sauté over medium heat for 2 to 3 minutes. Add the rice and water; bring to a boil. Reduce the heat, cover, and simmer for 20 minutes, or until the rice is cooked.

Serves 10 to 12

Yellow Rice with Green Pigeon Peas
(*Arroz con Gandules*)

This is our national rice-and-bean dish. It is a must during the Christmas season!

          2 **tablespoons annatto oil (see page 8)**
          ¼ **cup sliced *chorizo* (red Spanish sausage)**
          ¼ **cup diced smoked ham**
          ¾ **cup Basic *Recaíto* (see page 16)**
          1 **can (about 16 ounces) *gandules* (green pigeon peas), or 1 14-ounce bag frozen**
          2 **cups tomato sauce**
          2 **cups short-grain rice**
    4 to 4½ **cups water**
             Salt and black pepper to taste

Heat the oil in a large pot with a tight-fitting lid. Add the *chorizo* and smoked ham and fry lightly. Add the *recaíto*, *gandules*, and tomato sauce. Mix well and cook over medium heat for 5 minutes. Add the rice and water to cover. Turn the heat to medium-high and cook until the water is entirely absorbed. Add salt and pepper, stir, and turn the heat to low. Cover and cook for 30 to 45 minutes.

To serve, turn the rice out onto a platter. Scrape off the crusty layer that will have formed at the bottom of the pan, and top the rice with it.

Serves 4

TRADITIONAL DRIED BEANS

Type of Bean (1 Cup Dry)	Approximate Cooking Time	Yield (in Cups)
Black	45 min.	2⅓
Black-eyed peas	25 to 30 min.	2½
Cannellini (white)	45 min.	2½
Garbanzo (chick-peas)	55 min.	2½
Great Northern (white)	1 hour	2½
Green peas	1 hour, 15 min.	2½
Lentils	15 to 20 min.	3
Lima (small)	25 to 30 min.	2½
Lima (large)	1 hour	2½
Lowfield peas	30 min.	3
Navy (small white)	45 min.	2½
Pigeon peas (*gandules*)	1 hour	2½
Pink	50 to 55 min.	2½
Pinto	45 to 50 min.	2½
Red kidney (small)	1 hour	2⅓
Red kidney (large)	45 min.	2
Roman	35 to 40 min.	2⅓

BOUTIQUE DRIED BEANS

Type of Bean (1 Cup Dry)	Approximate Cooking Time	Yield (in Cups)
Adzuki	30 to 45 min.	3
Appaloosa	50 min.	4
Black soybeans	2 hours	2½
Calypso	1 hour, 40 min.	3½
Cargamanto	1 hour, 50 min.	3
Christmas lima	1 hour	4
Cranberry	1½ to 2 hours	2½
European soldier	1½ hours	4
Jacob's cattle	1¼ hours	3½
Low's champion	1½ hours	3
Rice	½ hour	3
Snow cap	45 min. to 1 hour	5½
Tongues of fire	45 min.	3½

NOTE: Packages of these beans can vary from ½ pound to 1 pound. These beans, except for black soybeans and adzukis, do not require soaking.

Black soybeans need at least 12 hours of soaking. Start with boiling hot water and change it once or twice to prevent the beans from beginning to ferment (sour).

Traditional Dried Bean Stew
(Habichuelas Secas Guisadas Tradicionales)

You can use any of the beans used in traditional Puerto Rican cookery in this tasty stew.

> 1 tablespoon annatto oil (see page 8) combined with 1 tablespoon olive oil
> ½ pound smoked ham, diced
> 1 *chorizo* (red Spanish sausage), sliced
> ¼ cup Basic *Recaíto* (see page 16)
> 1½ cups tomato sauce
> 1½ cups water or chicken stock
> ¼ pound *calabaza* (West Indian pumpkin) or potatoes, peeled and diced
> ¼ cup *alcaparrado*
> 3 cups cooked beans (see page 160)
> ½ teaspoon black pepper

Heat the oil in a large pot. Add the ham and *chorizo* and sauté over medium heat for 2 to 3 minutes. Add the *recaíto* and tomato sauce. Cook for 5 minutes. Add the water, *calabaza*, and *alcaparrado*. Bring the mixture to a boil.

Reduce the heat to a simmer and cook for 10 minutes. Add the beans and black pepper and turn the heat to medium-low. Cook for 10 minutes more.

Serves 6

NOTE: To make a bean stew that combines Cuban and Puerto Rican cookery, use 1½ cups cooked *gandules* (green pigeon peas) and 1½ cups cooked black beans.

Quick Bean Stew
(*Habichuelas Guisadas Rapiditas*)

Traditional flavor is combined with the modern convenience of canned beans.

- 2 tablespoons olive oil
- ¼ pound smoked ham, diced
- ¼ cup Basic *Recaíto* (see page 16)
- 1 cup tomato sauce
- 2 cups water or chicken stock
- ¼ pound *calabaza* (West Indian pumpkin), peeled and diced
- 1 cup *alcaparrado*
- 2 16-ounce cans beans, drained and rinsed
- 1 teaspoon black pepper

Heat the oil in a large pot. Sauté the ham for 3 minutes. Add the *recaíto* and tomato sauce, and cook over medium heat for 5 minutes. Add the water and *calabaza*. Bring to a boil, and add the *alcaparrado*, beans, and black pepper. Bring to a boil again. Reduce the heat and simmer, uncovered, for 15 minutes.

Serves 6

Five-Bean Stew
(Cinco Habichuelas Guisadas)

All the beans that are used daily on the island are combined here, in case you can't decide which ones you like best!

1 recipe Traditional Dried Bean Stew (see page 174) using:
½ cup cooked *gandules* (green pigeon peas)
1 cup cooked pink beans
½ cup cooked small white beans
½ cup cooked small red beans
½ cup cooked chick-peas

Serves 6

Mamposteao Rice
(*Arroz Mamposteao*)

In the old days, mamposteao *rice was leftover white rice and bean stew combined with fresh herbs and spices. Today it is made from scratch and served at fine dining establishments on the island.*

> 2 tablespoons corn oil
> ¼ cup diced green bell pepper
> 2 garlic cloves, peeled and chopped
> 1 tablespoon chopped cilantro
> 1 cup any bean stew (see recipes, pages 174–176)
> 3 tablespoons tomato sauce
> 3 cups cooked rice

Heat the oil in a large pot. Sauté the green pepper, garlic, and cilantro over medium heat for 3 minutes. Add the beans and tomato sauce. Cook for 2 more minutes. Add the rice and cook, stirring constantly, for 5 more minutes.

Serves 6

Calypso Beans and Rice
(Arroz y Habichuelas Calipso)

This is a variation of Mamposteao *Rice (see page 177) with a touch of curry.*

  1 **tablespoon butter**
  2 **tablespoons olive oil**
  3 **cups cooked rice**
  3 **cups cooked calypso beans**
    Salt to taste
    Curry powder to taste

Heat the butter and oil in a large skillet. Add the rice and beans. Sauté over medium-high heat for 5 minutes. Season to taste.

Serves 6 to 8

NOTE: If calypso beans are unavailable use pink, black, or your favorite bean.

Orzo and Barley Pilaf
(Pilaf de Orzo y Cebada)

Orzo (Greek pasta) and barley combined make an excellent substitute for everyday white rice.

  2 tablespoons butter
  1 tablespoon olive oil
  1½ cups cooked orzo
  1½ cups cooked barley
      Salt and pepper to taste

Heat the butter and oil in a large skillet. Sauté the orzo and barley over medium heat for 5 minutes. Season with salt and pepper.

Serves 6

NOTE: For a dramatic presentation, prepare a bean stew with a boutique bean like calypso and serve it with this simple but flavorful pilaf.

Puerto Rican Cannelloni Minés Style
(Canelones Puertorriqueños al Estilo de Minés)

During my college years I lived in a boardinghouse where I received cooking lessons from Minés, the owner. She was an excellent cook and kept us well fed, especially during midterm days. This cannelloni dish was one of her specialties.

SAUCE

2 tablespoons olive oil
1 medium yellow onion, finely chopped
2 garlic cloves, peeled and finely chopped
1 medium Italian frying pepper, seeded and finely chopped
6 tablespoons tomato paste
4 cups tomato sauce
1 28-ounce can whole tomatoes, roughly chopped, with liquid
5 cups water
1 tablespoon salt
½ teaspoon black pepper
½ teaspoon sugar
½ teaspoon *Adobo* (see page 15)

BEEF PICADILLO STUFFING

3 pounds ground beef
1 cup manzanilla olives, chopped
1½ cups tomato paste
¾ cup Basic *Recaíto* (see page 16)
½ cup golden raisins
1 tablespoon salt
2 teaspoons black pepper

3 quarts water
¼ cup olive oil
18 pieces cannelloni
2 cups shredded mozzarella cheese

Heat the oil in a large pot. Sauté the onion, garlic, and Italian pepper until soft. Add the remaining sauce ingredients and bring to a boil. Reduce the heat to a simmer and cook for 2 hours, stirring occasionally and adding water as needed. Set aside.

Brown the ground beef in a skillet over medium heat. Drain any excess fat. Add the remaining stuffing ingredients and cook for 10 minutes. Set aside. In a big pot, bring the water and olive oil to a boil. Add the cannelloni and cook for 5 minutes. Drain and rinse in cold water.

Preheat the oven to 375°F. Stuff each cannelloni with 4 tablespoons of beef *picadillo*. Arrange them in a shallow baking pan. Pour the sauce over the pasta, and sprinkle the cheese on top. Bake for 30 to 45 minutes, or until the cheese is completely melted and slightly browned.

Serves 6

Desserts and Breads

(Postres y Panes)

Our national dessert is *flan*, the versatile caramel custard. Many other desserts are based on coconut. We also prepare bread pudding, *arroz con dulce* (rice pudding cooked with coconut and ginger), and fruit sherbets like tamarind and soursop.

New desserts use our tropical fruits in very creative ways. Now guava mousse and *piña colada* cake can be found on the menus in many restaurants.

Breads once were limited to Mallorca bread and banana bread. Baking was not a part of home cooking; bread was mostly purchased at a local bakery along with desserts like guava turnovers. Today, I love to experiment with many different breads, giving them all a Puerto Rican touch!

Note: *Flans* are often cooked in a *bain-marie:* The custard is poured into a mold and the mold is then set and cooked in a pan of very hot water. The water should come about halfway up the sides of the mold.

Basic Vanilla Custard
(Flan de Vainilla Básico)

Rosa Franco, who owns a flan *manufacturing company in Connecticut, showed me how to make this exquisite yet simple custard.*

½ **cup sugar**
4 **eggs**
1 **14-ounce can sweetened condensed milk**
1 **12-ounce can evaporated milk**
1 **tablespoon vanilla extract**
  Fresh mixed berries for garnish

In a small heavy saucepan, cook the sugar over low heat until caramel forms. Pour it into an 8-inch round mold. Set aside. In a bowl, beat the eggs until frothy. Add the condensed milk, evaporated milk, and vanilla; mix well with the eggs.

Pour the mixture into the caramelized mold. Cook on top of the stove in a *bain-marie* on medium-high heat (see page 183), partially covered, for 35 minutes. The *flan* is done when a toothpick inserted near the center comes out clean. Let it cool at room temperature. Refrigerate for at least 2 hours (or better, overnight) before serving.

To serve, invert the *flan* on a platter. Garnish on top with fresh berries.

Serves 8

Irma's Stovetop Custard
(Natilla de Irma)

A dear friend, Irma Rosario, prepared this simple dessert for me many years ago. I've added fresh raspberries and whipped cream.

- **1 cup heavy cream**
- **2 cups milk**
- **1 cup sugar**
- **3 eggs**
- **½ cup cornstarch**
- **2 pints fresh raspberries**
- **Ground nutmeg for garnish**

Whip the cream and set aside. Combine the milk, sugar, eggs, and cornstarch in a blender or food processor. Pour into a saucepan and cook over low heat, stirring constantly, until the mixture coats the back of a spoon (about 15 to 20 minutes).

Pour the custard into a 9-inch baking pan and let it cool at room temperature. Transfer to the refrigerator until completely chilled. Arrange layers of custard, whipped cream, and raspberries in 6 glasses. Sprinkle with nutmeg.

Serves 6

NOTE: You can substitute sliced papaya, mango, or kiwi for berries.

Pumpkin Custard
(Flan de Calabaza)

Flan, *a dessert of our Spanish heritage, made with* calabaza *(West Indian pumpkin), results in a sophisticated dessert.*

½ **cup sugar**
1½ **pounds** *calabaza* **(West Indian pumpkin), peeled and diced**
   Water for boiling pumpkin
4 **eggs**
1 **12-ounce can evaporated milk**
1 **14-ounce can sweetened condensed milk**
1 **tablespoon vanilla extract**
   Pinch ground cinnamon

Heat the sugar carefully in a heavy saucepan until it caramelizes. Pour the caramel into a round 8-inch pan; set aside. Boil the pumpkin in the water until tender, about 15 to 20 minutes. Drain and purée in a blender or food processor.

Beat the eggs lightly in a large bowl. Add the remaining ingredients and mix well. Pour the *flan* mixture into the caramelized saucepan. Cook on top of the stove in a *bain-marie* (see page 183), covered, for 30 minutes over medium heat. Let the *flan* cool at room temperature. Turn upside down onto a platter.

Serves 8

Stovetop Coffee Flan
(Flan de Café Hecho en la Estufa)

My cousin Osvaldo taught me how to make flan *in a* bain-marie *on the stove. This coffee* flan *is one of my son Alex's favorites.*

⅓ **cup plus 2 tablespoons sugar**
4 **eggs**
1 **cup evaporated milk, undiluted**
1 **cup sweetened condensed milk**
¼ **teaspoon salt**
½ **cup strongly brewed black coffee**

In a small heavy saucepan, cook the ⅓ cup of sugar over low heat until it caramelizes. Pour into a 2-quart mold; set aside. In a large bowl, beat the eggs until frothy. Add the remaining ingredients and strain through a fine sieve. Pour the custard mix into the caramelized mold. Cook on top of the stove in a *bain-marie* (see page 183), on medium-high heat, covered, for 25 minutes. Let the *flan* cool at room temperature. Refrigerate for 2 hours before transferring to a serving platter.

Serves 6 to 8

Coconut Custard
(Tembleque)

Called tembleque *(the word translates as "shaky"), this custard has a jellylike consistency. This recipe can also be prepared in a 1-quart mold. It can be made the day before it is served.*

**3 cups fresh coconut milk, or unsweetened canned
  coconut milk**
½ cup sugar
¼ cup cornstarch

Blend all of the ingredients well in a blender or food processor. Transfer to a saucepan. Bring to a boil, stirring constantly. Reduce the heat and simmer until the custard coats the back of a spoon, about 4 minutes.

Pour the custard into 6 glass custard cups. Cover with plastic wrap to prevent a skin from forming. Refrigerate until firm, about 4 hours or overnight.

Serves 6

Coconut Custard with Mango Sauce
(Tembleque con Salsa de Mango)

The mango sauce not only adds flavor to the tembleque; *it also adds color.*

1 recipe Coconut Custard (see page 188)
2 medium mangoes, peeled, seeded, puréed, and pressed through a strainer to remove fibers
2 tablespoons golden rum or spiced rum

Unmold the coconut custard onto a platter. Combine the mango and rum. Pour the sauce over the custard.

Serves 6

Coconut Kisses
(Besitos de Coco)

These delicious dessert "cookies," served on sea-grape leaves, are sold at the Luquillo Beach kioskos.

2 cups grated fresh coconut (the meat of 1 medium-size coconut)
1 cup water
1½ cups dark brown sugar

Combine the coconut and water in a saucepan with a heavy bottom. Bring to a boil. Add the brown sugar. Reduce the heat to low and cook for 30 minutes, stirring occasionally, or until the mixture becomes thick and sticky. Drop the mixture by tablespoons onto a greased cookie sheet. Let the coconut kisses cool completely.

Makes 18 "kisses"

NOTE: Use a measuring spoon to keep the "kisses" uniform in size.

Coconut-Guava Cookies
(*Galletitas de Coco y Guayaba*)

These are a variation of the traditional polvorones. *You can replace the guava preserves with other jams such as raspberry, papaya, or mango.*

  1 **cup (2 sticks) unsalted butter at room temperature**
  ½ **cup sugar**
  ½ **cup sweetened flaked coconut**
  ½ **teaspoon vanilla extract**
  ¾ **cup guava preserves**

In a large bowl, beat the butter and sugar until fluffy. Blend in the coconut and vanilla extract. Refrigerate until the dough is firm, about ½ hour.

Preheat the oven to 350°F. Shape each tablespoon of dough into a ball. Arrange them on an ungreased baking sheet, 1 inch apart. Make a small indentation in the center of each cookie with your thumb. Bake the cookies until they are lightly browned around the edges, about 15 minutes. Let them cool on a rack. Fill each indentation with guava preserves.

Makes 3½ dozen

Edgar's Bread Pudding with Fruit Cocktail

(Pudín Diplomático de Edgar)

This is bread pudding with fruit cocktail added, the dessert we serve on special occasions. Edgar, my son's godfather, always serves it at dinner parties.

1 pound sliced white bread, cut into small pieces
1 cup milk
½ cup coconut milk
3 eggs
½ cup sugar
1 tablespoon vanilla extract
2 cups fruit cocktail in light syrup, drained
  Butter to grease baking pan
  Ground cinnamon for garnish

Preheat the oven to 350°F. In a large bowl, combine the two milks and mix with the bread. Set aside. In a separate bowl, beat the eggs, sugar, and vanilla and mix in the fruit cocktail. Add the egg mixture to the bread.

Grease a 9-inch baking pan and pour in the bread mixture. Bake for 50 minutes, or until a toothpick inserted in the center comes out clean. Cool at room temperature. Sprinkle with cinnamon.

Serves 12 to 15

Passion Fruit Bread Pudding
(Budín de Pan con Parcha)

This is our traditional bread pudding, with a touch of passion fruit.

1 pound sliced white bread, cut into small cubes
½ cup golden raisins
4 eggs
½ cup sugar
¾ cup evaporated milk
¾ cup milk
¾ cup sweetened condensed milk
1 cup frozen passion fruit juice concentrate, thawed
Butter to grease a 9-inch baking pan

Preheat the oven to 350°F. Combine the bread pieces and raisins in a bowl; set aside. In a separate bowl, mix all of the remaining ingredients well. Pour over the bread, making sure everything is well combined.

Grease the baking pan and pour the bread mixture into it. Bake for 50 minutes, or until a toothpick inserted in the center comes out clean. Cool at room temperature. Refrigerate for at least 1 hour before serving, or overnight if possible.

Serves 12 to 15

Puerto Rican Rice Pudding
(Arroz con Dulce)

This pudding is one of the traditional Christmas desserts. Fresh ginger and coconut distinguish it from the American version.

Islanders use regular brown raisins. I prefer currants for an elegant touch.

3 cups water
1 teaspoon salt
2 cinnamon sticks
6 whole cloves
1 1-inch piece fresh ginger, peeled and sliced
1 14-ounce can coconut milk
1 cup water
1 cup short-grain rice
⅓ cup dried currants or raisins
4 tablespoons shredded sweetened coconut
½ cup sugar
   Ground cinnamon for garnish

In a large saucepan, combine the 3 cups water, salt, cinnamon sticks, cloves, and ginger. Bring to a boil. Pour the liquid through a colander into a bowl; discard the spices.

Combine the spiced water with the coconut milk and 1 cup water in a large saucepan. Bring the liquid to a boil. Add all the remaining ingredients except the cinnamon. Reduce the heat, cover, and simmer for 20 minutes. Remove the lid from the pan, stir, and cook for 15 more minutes, or until the rice is cooked. (All the liquid should be absorbed.) Pour onto a platter and sprinkle with cinnamon.

Serves 6 to 8

NOTE: For a fruity variation, add 1 cup of diced mango during the last 5 minutes of cooking.

Ginger and Soursop Sorbet
(*Sorbete de Gengibre y Guanábana*)

I miss fresh soursop so much that I try to adapt every recipe to the frozen pulp available here in the States. This simple sorbet gets the right touch with the addition of fresh ginger. Sit back and enjoy a little piece of the Caribbean right here at home!

>   3 cups frozen soursop pulp, thawed
>   1 cup sugar
>   ½ cup Spiced Rum (see page 226)
>   3½ teaspoons grated fresh ginger
>   2 tablespoons fresh lemon juice

Process the soursop pulp in a blender or food processor. Pass through a sieve and return it to the blender or food processor. Add the remaining ingredients and purée. Freeze in an ice cream maker according to the manufacturer's instructions. To serve, let the sorbet sit at room temperature until it begins to soften.

Makes 1 quart

NOTE: If you don't have an ice cream machine, pour the mixture into a metal baking pan. Cover with aluminum foil and freeze until firm.

Mango and Passion Fruit Frozen Yogurt
(Yogurt Congelado de Mango y Parcha)

A more refreshing and mouth-watering frozen dessert is hard to imagine!

4 **medium mangoes, peeled and cubed**
1 **cup passion fruit pulp**
⅓ **cup sugar**
½ **teaspoon vanilla extract or more to taste**
1½ **cups plain yogurt**

In a food processor or blender, purée the mango, then strain through a sieve. Add the remaining ingredients. Pour the mixture into a shallow square 9-inch baking pan. Cover with foil or plastic wrap. Freeze until solid (1 to 2 hours). Break the frozen mixture into pieces. Purée until soft but not completely melted. Repeat the freezing and processing once or twice more. Serve or return to the freezer for later use.

Makes 4½ cups

Guava Mousse
(Mousse de Guayaba)

This mousse can be served immediately or frozen for later use.

     6 **egg whites**
  1½ **cups sugar**
  1½ **cups heavy cream**
     1 **cup frozen guava pulp, thawed**

Beat the egg whites and sugar in a large bowl until stiff peaks form. In a separate bowl, whip the heavy cream until soft peaks form. Fold the whipped cream and guava into the egg whites, in alternating batches.

Serves 6 to 8

Piña Colada Cake
(Bizcocho de Piña Colada)

Coconut milk and pineapple, classic ingredients in the famous piña colada, *are combined here to produce a delicate dessert. This cake can be accentuated with a raspberry sauce. It is best to let the cake soak overnight in the coconut syrup.*

1½ cups coconut milk
½ cup coconut cream
3 tablespoons dark rum
¼ cup canned crushed pineapple, drained
1 cup confectioners' sugar
⅔ cup ground almonds (about 3 ounces)
⅓ cup all-purpose flour
4 egg whites
3 drops almond extract
3 drops vanilla extract
¼ pound (1 stick) unsalted butter or margarine
Butter to grease the custard cups
Shredded sweetened coconut for garnish

Combine the coconut milk and cream in a saucepan. Bring to a boil. Lower the heat and simmer until the liquid is reduced to 1 cup. Add the rum and set aside. Grease 4 custard cups and divide the pineapple evenly among them. Set aside.

Combine the sugar, almonds, and flour in a bowl. Add the egg whites and extracts and whisk until the mixture is smooth. Preheat the oven to 375°F. Melt the butter in a saucepan over medium heat until it turns brown, then add to the batter. Divide the batter evenly among the 4 custard cups, making sure to cover the pineapple.

Bake for 20 minutes, or until the cakes are golden brown. Pour the coconut syrup over the hot cakes. Let them soak for at least 2 hours or overnight.

To serve, run a small knife around the sides of the cups to loosen the cakes. Turn them out onto a plate. Garnish with shredded coconut.

Serves 4

Soursop Terrine
(Terina de Guanábana)

A simple dessert, ideal for a hot summer day!

2 cups frozen soursop pulp, thawed
2 envelopes plain gelatin
1 cup heavy cream, whipped
Fresh kiwi slices for garnish

Purée the soursop pulp in a blender or food processor. Pass it through a sieve. Heat the pulp in a saucepan over medium heat and add the gelatin. Stir until it dissolves. Cool the pulp over iced water; fold in the whipped cream. Pour the mixture into an 8-inch round pan or a small bread pan. Refrigerate until the terrine is set. To serve, place the terrine briefly in a pan of hot water to loosen it. Turn it upside down on a platter and garnish with kiwi slices.

Serves 8

NOTE: You can serve this with a raspberry sauce.

White Cheese and Fruit Salad
with
Lemon-Honey Dressing
(Ensalada de Queso Blanco y Frutas con Salsa de Miel y Limón)

This light and refreshing salad is the perfect end to a summer brunch.

1 ripe papaya
2 medium ripe mangoes
1 small ripe pineapple
½ cup fresh lemon juice
4 tablespoons honey
1 pound Puerto Rican white cheese, cut into small pieces
Fresh mint sprigs for garnish

Peel the fruit and cut it into chunks. Combine the lemon juice and honey; pour over the fruit. Toss well. Divide the fruit and cheese among 6 bowls. Garnish with mint.

Serves 6

Tropical Gazpacho Fruit Soup
(Gazpacho Tropical de Frutas)

This bubbly fruit gazpacho combines sparkling water with tropical fruits. It makes a refreshing cold dessert soup.

3   cups fresh or frozen raspberries
3   cups sparkling water
½   cup sugar
    Juice of 1 lemon
1   papaya, peeled and cut into small pieces
1   medium mango, peeled, seeded, and diced
2   kiwis, peeled and diced
1   cup fresh pineapple pieces
    Shredded fresh ginger to taste for garnish

Purée the raspberries in a blender or food processor. Pass through a sieve to remove the seeds. In a nonreactive bowl, combine the raspberry *purée* with the sparkling water and sugar. Add the remaining ingredients except the ginger. Refrigerate for 1 hour before serving. Garnish with the ginger.

Serves 6 to 8

Sautéed Bananas with Orange Liqueur
(Guineos Salteados con Licor de China)

Bananas cooked in butter, sugar, and orange liqueur make a delicious topping for vanilla ice cream.

3 tablespoons butter
1 tablespoon brown sugar
1 tablespoon orange liqueur
3 medium bananas, sliced in half and cut into 1-inch
    pieces
1 quart vanilla ice cream
    Shredded sweetened coconut and chopped walnuts for
    garnish

Melt the butter in a saucepan over medium heat. Add the brown sugar and orange liqueur. Sauté the bananas until lightly golden. Divide them among 6 dessert bowls. Put a scoop of ice cream in each bowl. Sprinkle with coconut and walnuts.

Serves 6

Honey-Rum Mousse
(Mousse de Miel y Ron)

This is a very rich and delicious dessert that is simple to make and perfect for warm weather.

6 egg yolks, at room temperature
⅓ cup honey
1 cup whipping cream, chilled
2 tablespoons Spiced Rum (see page 226)

Beat the yolks and honey in a bowl until they have the stiff texture of meringue (about 10 minutes). In another bowl, beat the cream and rum until the mixture forms soft peaks. Fold the two mixtures together. Spoon into 6 custard cups.

Serves 6

NOTE: You can also freeze this dessert and serve it later.

Guava Cheesecake
(Bizcocho de Crema con Guayaba)

This cheesecake is easy to make. The intense guava flavor makes it quite rich.

CRUST

4 ounces vanilla wafers, crushed
2 tablespoons butter, melted

FILLING

1½ pounds cream cheese, softened
6 eggs
1 cup frozen guava juice concentrate, thawed
3 tablespoons sugar
4 tablespoons all-purpose flour
1 18-ounce can guava shells, drained and cut into thin
     slices, for garnish (optional)
   Fresh mint leaves for garnish

Preheat the oven to 400°F. Combine the vanilla wafer crumbs with the melted butter. Press into a 10- or 12-inch springform pan. Refrigerate while you prepare the filling.

In a food processor or with an electric beater, beat the cream cheese until it is fluffy. Add the eggs one at a time. Continue beating until the eggs are well incorporated into the cream cheese and the mixture is light. Add the guava concentrate, sugar, and flour, and beat until well mixed.

Pour the batter into the pan. Bake for 1½ hours, or until a knife inserted in the center comes out clean. (If the top starts to brown too quickly, place a piece of aluminum foil loosely on top.) Cool at room temperature. Refrigerate for at least 1 hour before serving, or overnight. To serve, arrange the guava-shell slices and mint leaves on top of the cake.

Serves 8 to 10

Puerto Rican Jelly Roll

(Brazo Gitano al Estilo Puertorriqueño)

Jelly roll filled with guava preserves is a favorite traditional Puerto Rican dessert. You can use mango, papaya, or passion fruit jellies, jams, or preserves.

　2　**tablespoons vegetable shortening**
　1　**9 × 15-inch piece of parchment paper**
⅓　**cup egg yolks (about 8 yolks)**
1¼　**cups egg whites**
1¼　**cups sugar**
　1　**teaspoon salt**
⅔　**cup milk**
1¼　**cups cake flour**
¾　**tablespoon baking powder**
¾　**cup guava preserves**
　　Confectioners' sugar for garnish

Preheat the oven to 350°F. Grease a 9 × 15-inch sheet pan with vegetable shortening. Place the parchment paper on the baking sheet and grease well. Set aside.

Beat the egg yolks and whites, sugar, and salt at high speed until stiff peaks form. While the eggs are beating, scald the milk and cool briefly.

Fold the flour and baking powder into the egg mixture. Add the scalded milk and blend thoroughly. Spread the batter evenly onto the parchment-covered sheet pan. Bake for 8 minutes, or until lightly browned.

Remove the cake from the pan by lifting the paper. Let it cool on a rack for 5 minutes. Spread the marmalade evenly over the entire surface of the cake.

Gently loosen the cake from the parchment paper and roll it tightly from the short end. Sprinkle with confectioners' sugar.

Serves 4 to 6

Rum Cake

(Bizcocho de Ron)

Spiced rum and honey flavor this cake. Serve it with whipped cream and chopped nuts.

¼ **pound (1 stick) butter or margarine, at room
     temperature**
¼ **cup brown sugar**
¼ **cup honey**
2 **eggs**
¼ **cup water**
½ **cup Spiced Rum (see page 226)**
2 **cups cake flour, sifted**
2½ **teaspoons baking powder**
¼ **teaspoon salt**
  Butter to grease pan
  Confectioners' sugar for garnish

Preheat the oven to 350°F. Cream the butter and brown sugar in a large bowl. Add the honey, eggs, water, and rum. Mix well.

In another bowl, combine the cake flour, baking powder, and salt. Pour over the creamed mixture and beat until all of the ingredients are combined. Grease an 8-inch round pan and pour in the batter. Bake for 30 minutes, or until a knife inserted in the center comes out clean. Let the cake cool in the pan or on a cooling rack.

To serve, invert the cake onto a platter. (Trim the top if uneven.) Sift confectioners' sugar on top.

Serves 8

Orange and Papaya Tart
(Tarta de China y Papaya)

Papaya and orange are combined in this simple dessert.

1 **pound frozen puff pastry, thawed**
  Flour for dusting
  Grated peel of 1 orange
1 **1-pound bag beans (to prebake the tart pastry)**
1 **large papaya, peeled, seeded, and sliced**
¼ **cup apricot preserves**
1 **teaspoon honey**

Preheat the oven to 400°F. Roll out the puff pastry to ¼ inch thick. Dust with flour. Place the pastry in a 10-inch tart pan with a removable bottom; trim the edges. Prick the pastry all over with a fork, and sprinkle orange peel over the dough. Place a sheet of aluminum foil over the pastry. Distribute the beans evenly over the foil to create some weight. Bake for 15 minutes. Remove the beans and foil. Continue baking for another 30 minutes, or until the puff pastry is golden brown and completely cooked. Cool at room temperature.

Arrange the papaya slices on the pastry. In a saucepan over medium-low heat, warm the apricot preserves and honey. Strain and let cool. Brush the tart with the apricot mixture.

Serves 6 to 8

Almond Cookies
(Polvorones)

I first heard about these cookies during my junior-high-school years. They were a specialty of Lizzie Morales, one of my classmates. Serve them with tea or café con leche.

- **1 egg yolk**
- **½ cup sugar**
- **½ cup (1 stick) butter**
- **1 teaspoon almond extract**
- **1½ cups all-purpose flour**

Preheat the oven to 350°F. Beat the egg yolk, sugar, butter, and almond extract in a large bowl. Blend in the flour a little at a time. Shape a tablespoon of dough into a ball. Repeat with the remaining dough. Place the cookies on an ungreased cookie sheet. Bake for 20 minutes, or until light golden brown.

Makes 22 polvorones

Guava Turnovers
(Pastelillos de Guayaba)

These are eaten with café con leche *as an afternoon snack. They can also be served for dessert. I like to sprinkle cinnamon and nutmeg on the dough.*

All-purpose flour for dusting
1 **pound frozen puff pastry, thawed and cut into 4-inch squares**
   Ground cinnamon and nutmeg to taste
1 **cup canned guava preserves (not guava paste)**
1 **egg, beaten**
   Butter to grease cookie sheet
   Parchment paper

Preheat the oven to 350°F. Dust your working surface with flour. Roll out the puff pastry to make a rectangle measuring 8 × 16 inches. Sprinkle cinnamon and nutmeg on the dough. Put 1½ tablespoons guava preserves in each piece of puff pastry. Brush the edges with beaten egg. Fold over to form a triangle.

Grease a cookie sheet and line with parchment paper. Place the pastries 2 inches apart. Refrigerate for 30 minutes. Bake for 25 to 30 minutes, or until light golden brown. Cool before serving.

Makes 8 to 10 pastries

Banana Bread
(Pan de Guineo)

A simple bread, packed with banana flavor.

 3 **very ripe bananas**
 ½ **cup sugar**
 ½ **cup (1 stick) butter**
 3 **eggs**
 ½ **teaspoon salt**
 2 **cups all-purpose flour**
 1 **teaspoon baking powder combined with 2 tablespoons**
     sour cream
     Butter to grease pan

Preheat the oven to 350°F. In a large bowl, mash the bananas. Add the sugar, butter, and eggs. Beat until well blended. In a separate bowl, sift the salt and flour together. Combine with the banana mixture. Add the baking powder–sour cream mix.

Grease an 8-inch pan and pour the batter into it. Bake for 30 minutes, or until a toothpick inserted in the center comes out clean.

Serves 6 to 8

Mallorca Bread
(Pan de Mallorca)

The perfect afternoon coffee break is a steaming hot cup of café con leche *and a* pan de mallorca.

The traditional bread is somewhat complicated and time-consuming to prepare. Through the years I have tried different ways to make this delicious bread in a reasonable amount of time and a less complicated fashion. Here is my final version.

> 6 tablespoons (¾ stick) butter
> 1 package active dry yeast
> ¼ cup lukewarm water
> ¼ cup sugar
> ¾ teaspoon salt
> 3 egg yolks
> ½ cup milk
> 2½ to 3 cups all-purpose flour
>   Flour for dusting work surface
>   Butter to grease bowl and pan
>   Confectioners' sugar for dusting

Melt the butter and let it cool slightly. In a large bowl, dissolve the yeast in the water. Add the sugar, salt, egg yolks, milk, 4 tablespoons of the cooled butter, and 2½ cups of the flour. Mix well. Lightly flour a work surface. Turn out the dough and knead for 5 minutes. Add enough of the remaining flour so that the dough is not sticky.

Grease a bowl with butter. Put the dough in it and cover with plastic wrap. Let the dough rise in a warm place for 45 minutes. Grease a 9-inch square baking pan. Set aside. Punch the dough down. Knead it on a lightly floured surface into a rectangle about 18 × 9 inches. Brush with the remaining melted butter. Roll up the dough from one short end and cut it into 9 slices; trim the ends to make them neat. Arrange the slices in the baking pan. Cover and let rise for 40 minutes.

Preheat the oven to 375°F. Bake the rolls for 30 minutes, or until lightly browned. Let the rolls cool in the pan for 5 minutes. Transfer to a platter and dust with confectioners' sugar.

Makes 9 rolls

Carnival Corn Bread
(Pan de Maíz de Carnaval)

Food festivals have become popular on the island over the past ten years. In 1991 I went to the mabí *festival in Juana Díaz. Street vendors were offering different versions of the drink the town is most famous for:* mabí, *a drink made of fermented tree bark that tastes a bit like root beer. There were also tables with traditional and new dishes. A corn bread made with carrots caught my attention.*

1   **cup sifted all-purpose flour**
1   **cup yellow cornmeal**
¼   **cup sugar (or less to taste)**
1   **tablespoon baking powder**
1   **teaspoon salt**
¼   **cup (½ stick) butter or margarine, softened**
1   **egg**
1   **cup plain or vanilla yogurt**
2   **medium carrots, peeled and shredded**
½   **cup fresh, canned, or frozen corn kernels**
    Butter to grease pan

Preheat the oven to 425°F. Sift the flour, cornmeal, sugar, baking powder, and salt into a bowl. Cut in the butter until the mixture forms little balls the size of peas.

In a separate bowl, beat the egg until frothy. Add the yogurt, carrots, and corn. Combine with the dry ingredients. Pour into a greased loaf pan. Bake for 20 minutes, or until a toothpick inserted in the center comes out dry. Cool in the pan.

Serves 10 to 12

Campobello Bread
(Pan Campobello)

This semisweet corn-and-banana bread is ideal for brunches or picnics. Serve it with eggs and sausages.

2 large bananas
¼ cup (½ stick) butter, melted
2 tablespoons honey
1 cup all-purpose flour
1 cup yellow cornmeal
2 teaspoons baking powder
½ teaspoon salt
½ cup fresh, canned, or frozen corn kernels
   Butter to grease pan

Preheat the oven to 350°F. Purée the bananas in a blender or food processor. Add the butter and honey and process again. In a large bowl, sift together all of the dry ingredients. Stir in the banana purée. Pour into a greased 8-inch baking pan. Bake for 30 minutes, or until a toothpick inserted in the center comes out clean.

Serves 6 to 8

13

DRINKS AND BEVERAGES
Bebídas y Refrescos

As the main producer of rum in the world, we have very interesting drinks in addition to our famous *piña coladas*. Rum and (occasionally) flavored liqueurs are combined with traditional fruit juices. There are also some very good and festive nonalcoholic drinks—the tastes are so good you won't miss the liquor!

Piña Colada

There are as many recipes for this drink, created on the island by Ramón Marrero, bartender at the Caribe Hilton Hotel, as there are people living in Puerto Rico. My version gets a splash of vanilla extract and uses coconut milk instead of the very sweet cream of coconut.

   2 **cups coconut milk**
   3 **cups pineapple juice**
   2 **cups crushed pineapple**
   ½ **cup shredded sweetened coconut**
   1 **cup golden rum**
   ½ **cup sugar**
   ½ **teaspoon vanilla extract or more to taste**
     About 2 cups ice cubes
     Fresh mint leaves for garnish

In a bowl, combine all of the ingredients except the ice and mint leaves. Mix in batches with the ice in a blender. Garnish with mint leaves.

Serves 10 to 12

Rum and Banana Colada
(*Guineo Colada con Ron*)

This is a twist on the classic piña colada. *It is made with fresh bananas and banana liqueur.*

¼ **cup white rum**
1 **banana, peeled and sliced**
¼ **cup banana liqueur**
¼ **cup cream of coconut**
  About 2 cups ice cubes
  Fresh mint leaves for garnish

Combine all of the ingredients, except the mint leaves, in a blender. Garnish with mint leaves.

Serves 2 to 4

Rum Collins

Move over gin! Here comes white rum and fresh lime juice.

¼ **cup golden rum (or more to taste)**
2 **tablespoons fresh lime juice**
1 **teaspoon sugar**
½ **cup club soda**
1 **orange slice for garnish**

Mix all of the ingredients except the orange slice. Pour into a glass filled with ice cubes. Garnish with the orange slice.

Serves 1

Old San Juan Daiquiri
(Daiquiri al Estilo del Viejo San Juan)

This is a daiquiri à la Puerto Rico—white rum mixed with guava nectar.

¼ **cup white rum**
½ **cup guava nectar**
   Dash grenadine syrup
1 **lime wedge**

Pour all of the ingredients except the lime wedge into an iced-filled glass. Squeeze the lime wedge into the drink.

Serves 1

Puerto Rican Sangría
(Sangría Criolla)

The addition of rum and passion fruit makes this a very Puerto Rican sangría!

 1½ **cups frozen passion fruit pulp, thawed**
  2 **cups pineapple juice**
  ½ **cup fresh lemon juice**
  2 **cups lemon-lime soda**
  2 **cups red wine**
  1 **cup white rum**
  1 **6-ounce can mandarin oranges**
     Ice cubes

Combine all of the ingredients in a pitcher. Chill for at least 1 hour before serving.

Serves 10

Guava Hidden Treasure
(Tesoro de Guayaba Escondido)

Fresh guavas are available on the mainland for only a short time during the summer months, but guava nectar, with its perfumelike aroma, is available year-round. This drink will make you think guavas are made in heaven!

¼ **cup white rum**
¼ **cup guava nectar**
¼ **cup pineapple juice**
¼ **cup coconut cream**
    About 2 cups ice cubes
    Orange slices for garnish

Combine all of the ingredients except the orange slices in a blender. Pour into tall glasses. Garnish with orange slices.

Serves 2

Caribbean Kiss
(Beso Caribeño)

Strawberries, like a kiss from red lips, give the perfect touch to this inviting rum drink.

¼ cup white rum
1 tablespoon grenadine syrup
1 tablespoon sugar
5 fresh strawberries, sliced
4 ice cubes
  Juice of 1 lemon
2 tablespoons light cream or evaporated milk
  Grated coconut for garnish

Combine all of the ingredients except the coconut in a blender. Pour into a tall glass. Garnish with coconut.

Serves 1

Mango Magic
(Magia de Mango)

When I first came to New York in 1981, it was very hard to find fresh mangoes. But in recent years they have become more abundant, and we have been lucky enough to enjoy them as early as February.

1 cup fresh mango pulp
¼ cup Triple Sec (or any other orange liqueur)
  About 2 cups ice cubes
¼ cup golden rum
1 tablespoon sugar
  Juice of 1 lime

Mix all of the ingredients in a blender. Serve well chilled.

Serves 4 to 6

Spiced Rum
(Ron con Especias)

This fragrant spiced rum can be used to soak dried fruits and to make desserts. Or simply add it to your after-dinner coffee.

- 1 **vanilla bean**
- 3 **cinnamon sticks**
- 6 **whole cloves**
- 4 **whole allspice**
- 1 **whole nutmeg, crushed**
- 3 **star anise**
  Pinch aniseed
- 1 **liter golden rum**

Make a slit along the vanilla bean. Scrape the pulp into a glass jar. Add the vanilla bean and the remaining ingredients and cover. Store the rum in a dry, cool place for at least 2 weeks. Strain and pour back into the rum bottle.

Makes 1 liter

Pineapple Liqueur
(*Licor de Piña*)

This is the perfect after-dinner drink to end a summer meal.

2½ cups fresh pineapple pieces
1½ cups white rum
1½ cups golden rum
1 teaspoon vanilla extract
½ cup simple sugar syrup (½ cup sugar with ¼ cup
    water, boiled)

Combine the pineapple, rums, and vanilla in a glass jar.
Cover and set aside in a dark place (inside a kitchen cabinet,
for instance) for 3 weeks; stir the mixture every 3 days. Drain,
reserving the liquid. Purée the pineapple in a blender or food
processor. Pass through a sieve lined with a coffee filter. Discard the pulp. Drain the liquid again through a coffee filter–
lined colander. Combine the remaining liquid and the
rum-vanilla liquid with the sugar syrup. Pour into a glass jar.

Makes 3 cups

Papaya Shake Siglo Veinte
(Batida de Papaya a lo Siglo Veinte)

Through the years El Siglo Veinte, a restaurant located on Fortaleza Street in Old San Juan, has been known for the delicious papaya shakes it prepares. Sipping one after a play at the Tapia Theater is a cherished tradition among Puerto Ricans.

I have added a touch of coffee liqueur. It can also be served as an unusual dessert following a light meal.

2 **ripe papayas, peeled, seeded, and diced**
4 **cups ice-cold milk**
4 **tablespoons coffee liqueur**
  Freshly ground nutmeg for garnish

Mix all of the ingredients except the nutmeg in a blender. Sprinkle with the nutmeg.

Serves 6 to 8

Passion Mimosa
(Parcha Mimosa)

Think of the patio of a parador *(country inn) and a glass of champagne combined with passion fruit. It is also a splendid way to start the Sunday brunch at home.*

1 **bottle champagne**
1 **quart passion fruit juice**
   Fresh fruit slices for garnish: oranges, strawberries, or kiwis

Fill 6 glasses two-thirds full with champagne. Add passion fruit juice and garnish with fresh fruit.

Serves 6

Rum Eggnog
(Coquito)

Coquito *is the traditional Christmas beverage in Puerto Rico. I learned to make it from my Aunt Celia. She would start preparing it at the beginning of December, and by the twenty-fifth the coquito would be what she called "cured." It is best if you use fresh coconut milk.*

    1 cup coconut milk
    1 cup sweetened condensed milk
    1 cup evaporated milk
    1 cup white rum, or to taste
    1 cup water
    3 cinnamon sticks
    4 egg yolks, well beaten
      Ground cinnamon for garnish

Combine all of the milks and the rum in a blender or a food processor. Set aside. Boil the water with the cinnamon sticks. Cool to room temperature. Discard the cinnamon sticks.

Combine all of the ingredients except the ground cinnamon and beat well in a blender or food processor in batches. Pour the eggnog into glass bottles and refrigerate until ready to use. To serve, transfer the eggnog to a punch bowl and sprinkle the cinnamon on top.

Makes 5 cups

Arturo's Christmas Punch
(Bul de Navidad a lo Arturo)

I prepared this recipe when Ralph Paniagua, publisher of the maga-zine Viva New York, *asked me to prepare a Christmas menu with a "new twist." Arturo Fortún, president of La Carta Publications, gave me this recipe.*

- 4 cups pineapple juice
- 4 cups orange juice (freshly squeezed, if possible)
- 1 cup fresh lemon juice
- 1 cup golden rum
- 1 lime, cut into small pieces
- ½ cup each fresh mango and papaya chunks (if mango is not available, use 1 cup of papaya)
  Ice cubes
  Fresh mint leaves for garnish

Combine all of the liquids in a punch bowl. Add the fruit, ice, and mint leaves. Serve well chilled.

Serves 10 to 12

Birthday Punch
(Bul de Cumpleaños)

On the island we celebrate a girl's fifteenth birthday much as mainland Americans celebrate the Sweet Sixteen. When the party takes place at home, a birthday punch is usually prepared.

2 cups each orange, grape, pineapple, and pear juice
3 cups beer
2 cups golden rum

Mix all of the ingredients. Serve icy cold in pitchers or a punch bowl.

Serves 12

NOTE: Some people like to add a can of fruit cocktail as a garnish.

Hot Rum Punch
(Bul de Ron Caliente)

This drink is a way of bringing island sunshine to your home on a cold winter night. This punch is perfect for holiday parties.

- **3 cups apple cider**
- **2 tablespoons sugar**
- **3 cinnamon sticks**
- **2 star anise**
- **5 whole cloves**
- **Pinch aniseed**
- **¼ cup fresh lemon juice**
- **¾ cup golden rum (or to taste)**
- **Lemon slices for garnish**

Heat the cider, sugar, and spices in a nonreactive pan over low heat for 5 minutes. Strain through a sieve. Add the lemon juice and rum. Place a lemon slice in each serving cup before pouring in the hot punch.

Serves 6 to 8

NOTE: You can use Spiced Rum (see page 226) to make this punch.

Basic Tropical Fruit Drink
(Refresco Tropical Básico)

You can prepare this delicious beverage with any tropical fruit: mamey, soursop, passion fruit, or guava.

Equal parts fruit pulp and water
Sugar to taste
Ice cubes

Combine all of the ingredients in a pitcher. Serve well chilled.

Villa Puerto Rico Passion Fruit and Raspberry Ginger Ale Cooler

(Villa Puerto Rico Parcha y Gingerale de Frambuesa)

Inspired by the bright yellow color of passion fruit, I created this drink and named it after one of the casitas, Villa Puerto Rico, which is painted bright yellow.

    4¼ cups raspberry ginger ale
    1½ cups passion fruit pulp
        Ice cubes
        Strawberry slices for garnish

Combine all of the ingredients except the strawberries. Serve well chilled, garnished with the strawberry slices.

Serves 6 to 8

Soursop and Milk Drink
(Champola de Guanábana)

When I was growing up, almost every backyard in my neighborhood had a guanábana *tree. My nanny, Delfa, used to give me this delicious drink as an after-school snack. The milk-and-cookie idea came to the island much later.*

3 **cups soursop pulp**
4 **cups milk**
1 **cup sugar, or to taste**
   Ice cubes
   Ground nutmeg for garnish

Combine all of the ingredients except the nutmeg in a pitcher. Refrigerate for 1 hour before serving. Sprinkle each glass with the nutmeg.

Serves 6 to 8

Orange Wine
(Vino de Chinas)

My Aunt Aurea used to serve a liqueur that she called "orange wine" at Christmas. This makes a good after-dinner drink.

2 cups white rum
  Juice of 10 oranges (save the oranges)
  Peel of 1 orange
1 cup sugar
3 cinnamon sticks
2 star anise
5 whole allspice
2 whole cloves
1 whole nutmeg, crushed
  Pinch aniseed
1 vanilla bean, chopped

Combine all of the ingredients, including the oranges, in a glass jar. Cover and let the mixture settle for 2 days. Shake the jar every night. Drain the liquid; refrigerate before serving.

Makes 5 cups

White Nonalcoholic Sangría
(Sangría sin Alcohol Blanca)

The summer of 1974 was very special for me. My mother (seven months pregnant with my brother) completed her bachelor's degree and I graduated from high school. To celebrate I created this nonalcoholic white sangría for her.

        4   **cups white grape juice**
        3   **cups sparkling water**
        1   **cup orange juice**
        1   **orange, cut in small pieces**
   4 to 5   **fresh strawberries, sliced**
            Ice cubes

Combine all of the ingredients in a pitcher. Refrigerate for 1 hour before serving.

Serves 8 to 10

Pineapple Punch
(Bul de Piña)

This is my favorite Easter Sunday drink.

- ½ **cup loosely packed mint leaves**
- 3 **cups pineapple juice**
- 3 **cups lemon-lime soda**
- 1 **orange, cut up in small pieces, for garnish**

Combine all of the ingredients in a pitcher. Serve well chilled.

Serves 6 to 8

GLOSSARY

a caballo   a folkloric expression that means a plate of rice and beans with a fried egg "mounted" on top.

aceite con achiote   annatto oil. (See "The Basics," page 8.)

aceite de maíz   corn oil. (See "The Basics," page 8.)

aceituna   olive. The olive most used in Puerto Rico is the manzanilla, which is a pitted green olive stuffed with pimiento.

acelga   Swiss chard. Used to make caldo Gallego (Galician soup).

acerola   West Indian or Barbados cherry. This fruit is best known for its high vitamin C content. Traditionally it was used to make *refresco de acerola*, or **acerola** juice.

achiote or **achote**   annatto seeds. (See "The Basics," page 8.)

achiotera   a container used to store annatto oil with its seeds. The oil is heated every time it is needed so the seeds can release their yellow color.

adobo   The basic seasoning combination of Puerto Rican cooking. (See "The Basics," page 8.)

aguacate   avocado.

agua de azahar   orange blossom water. A distilled water made of orange blossoms, used to flavor traditional desserts like rice-flour stovetop custard.

ají caballero or **ají picante**   hot chili pepper. A hot pepper about 1 inch long. It is the only hot pepper used in traditional cooking. It is also used to make *pique*, a fermented vinegar used as a condiment.

ají dulce   sweet chili pepper. (See "The Basics," page 8.)

ajilimójili   a traditional sauce made with garlic, peppercorns, oil, vinegar, and lemon juice. It is served with boiled root vegetables or over grilled meats.

ajo   garlic.

ajonjolí   sesame seeds.

alboronía de chayote   chayote salad.

alcaparra   caper. Most frequently used in **alcaparrado**.

alcaparrado   a mixture of green olives, capers, and pimientos. (See "The Basics," page 8.)

alcapurría   a traditional fritter made of grated **yautía** (taro root) and green bananas, stuffed with **picadillo**. It can also be stuffed with crabmeat or chicken.

almojábana   rice-flour fritter.

amarillo   ripe yellow plantain.

anafre   portable burner. Used in the old days in place of a stove. It was usually made of a cracker-tin can, with holes added to improve the ventilation. **Anafres** were also made of iron and placed on top of the **fogón**.

aní en semilla   aniseed. Used mostly to prepare desserts.

annatto   (See "The Basics," p. 8.)

apio   a root vegetable with brown skin, yellow flesh, and a very strong starchy taste. It is used mostly to make heavy soups like **sancocho** and tripe soup.

arroz   rice.

arroz amarillo   basic yellow rice made with annatto oil, which can also be combined with meat, seafood, or vegetables.

arroz con dulce   Puerto Rican rice pudding. A traditional dessert made with rice, coconut milk, ginger, and spices.

arroz con gandules   yellow rice with green pigeon peas. This is our national rice dish.

arroz con pollo   yellow rice with chicken.

arroz y habichuelas   rice and beans.

asalto Navideño   Christmas caroling. Traditionally, a group of people get together and surprise a neighbor in the middle of the night with Christmas songs. They go from house to house, and at the last stop they prepare a chicken **asopao**.

asopao   one of our national soups. It has a thick consistency and is derived from the Spanish **paella**. It is a mixture of rice, chicken, **alcaparrado** and **recaíto**. **Asopao** can also be made with seafood, green pigeon peas, or salt codfish.

avellana   hazelnut. Hazelnuts and walnuts are traditional Christmas nuts on the island.

bacalao   salt codfish. (See "The Basics," page 8.)

bacalaíto   salt codfish fritter.

barrilito   a type of Puerto Rican rum that is 86 proof.

batata, batata blanca   Puerto Rican yam or sweet potato. A root vegetable with a skin that varies from pink to purple. It has a gray-white flesh and a very sweet taste. **Batatas** are eaten boiled, baked, or fried.

berenjena eggplant.

besito de coco coconut kiss. A traditional dessert made with fresh-grated coconut, sugar, and spices.

bilí a mix of rum and **quenepas** that gets fermented. The rum is then drained and served. This is a typical drink of Vieques, an island located on the east coast of the island.

bistec cubed steak. Used to prepare Puerto Rican pepper steak.

bodega Spanish grocery store.

bollo de pan a loaf of bakery bread.

boronia de chayote **Chayote** stew.

buñuelo beignet a fritter made with flour, eggs, butter, and sugar. It can be sweet or savory (made with Parmesan cheese).

burén flat griddle. This was traditionally made of clay and used by the Taíno natives to cook **casabe**.

butifarra pork sausage seasoned with spices like cinnamon and anise, usually eaten for breakfast.

cabrito young goat. Usually prepared in a stew.

café coffee.

café con leche strong black coffee with steamed milk.

café negro black coffee.

café puya unsweetened black coffee.

café tinta espresso.

calabaza West Indian pumpkin. (See "The Basics," page 8.)

calamar en su tinta squid in its ink. Sold canned, it is used to make rice with squid.

caldero cauldron or cooking pot. This traditional pot, made of iron or thick aluminum, is used to make Puerto Rican rice dishes.

camarón   shrimp.

canela   cinnamon.

caña de azucar   sugar cane.

caramelo   caramel. Made of granulated sugar; used to coat the pan in which **flan** is cooked.

carne vieja   dry salted beef, sold in small slabs covered with a layer of lard. It is usually prepared with scrambled eggs and onions.

casabe   cassava bread. A flat bread made with grated cassava.

cascos de guayaba   guava shells. They are usually cooked in a sugar syrup and are readily available canned.

cazuela   a dessert casserole made of **calabaza** and yam.

champola   a soursop drink made with milk.

chayote   a vegetable of the squash family, also known as mirliton, vegetable pear, or christophine. It has a white or green skin and cream-colored flesh, with a somewhat bland taste. **Chayotes** can be stored at room temperature and are available year-round.

chicharrón   pork crackling. Deep-fried pieces of pork skin or cut-up pieces of boneless pork shoulder. Small pieces of deep-fried chicken are also called **chicharrón**. (See recipe, page 51.)

chillo   red snapper.

china   orange.

chironja   a cross between an orange and a grapefruit.

chorizo   Spanish sausage. Used to make yellow rice and found in braised meat dishes like **carne mechada** (pot roast).

cilantro   leaves of coriander. (See "The Basics," page 9.)

clavo   clove.

coco rallado   shredded coconut.

coco seco   dry, mature coconut with a brown, hairy shell and firm white flesh. (See "The Basics," page 9.)

coco verde   green coconut, usually sold refrigerated at roadside stands. The flesh is soft and the water, which is usually sweet, can be drunk straight from the coconut shell.

codito   elbow macaroni.

colador de café   cloth colander used in the old days to prepare coffee.

conejo   rabbit. Stewed rabbit meat is eaten on holidays and special occasions like weddings or christenings.

coquito   rum eggnog. This is a traditional Christmas drink.

crema de coco   coconut cream. (See "The Basics," page 9.)

criolla   creole. This term is used to denote traditional Puerto Rican cooking.

cuchifrito   deep-fried pork pieces sold at roadside stands. These usually consist of pig's ears, tails, stomach, etc. **Cuchifrito** is also the name given to the fast-food establishments on the island that serve traditional fritters to go.

culantro   is another name for **recao**. (See "The Basics," page 11.)

dita   a bowl carved from the *higuera* tree. In the old days it was used to wash rice and measure beans.

domplín   dumpling.

dulce   a sweet, usually eaten as a dessert, made with yam, pineapple, or coconut.

dulce de plátano   a dessert dish made with very ripe yellow plantains cooked in red wine, sugar, and spices.

empanada   turnover. A fritter made of dough stuffed with **picadillo**, crab stew, or chicken.

empanadilla   small turnover.

246

escabeche a pickling marinade traditionally prepared during the Lent season. Foods prepared **escabeche** style include salt codfish, chicken, green bananas, and fish.

fideo noodle.

filete beef tenderloin.

flan custard. A national dessert of Spanish heritage made of milk, eggs, sugar, and spices.

fogón a hearth made of three stones arranged in a triangle, with pieces of wood placed within.

fritura fritter.

funche Puerto Rican polenta. This has been a staple dish since the Taínos lived on the island. It used to be made with lard, but today corn or olive oil is used instead.

galleta por soda soda cracker. Eaten as an afternoon snack with **café con leche**. Crushed soda crackers, known as **galleta molida** (cracker meal), are used for breading.

gallina hen.

gandinza pork liver.

gandul green pigeon pea. (See "The Basics," page 9.)

garbanzo chick-pea.

granada pomegranate.

grano dialect term for rice-flour fritter on Puerto Rico's east coast, and the word for beans on some parts of the island.

greca de café Italian coffee pot used to make strong black coffee.

grosella gooseberry. Cooked in water and sugar to make a compote.

guanime Puerto Rican *tamal*. **Guanimes** have been a staple food since the Taíno days. They are made plain, without stuffing, and are wrapped in banana leaves. Served with salt cod-fish stew, **guanimes** are an everyday peasant lunch.

guarapo de caña sugar cane juice. Sold freshly squeezed at roadside stands.

guayaba guava. A fruit with a green skin, pink flesh, and small seeds. Fresh guavas are hard to find and can be expensive. Frozen pulp and juice concentrate are easily found year-round. On the island, where they are abundant, guavas are made into a paste and the shells are cooked in sugar syrup. Both are served as desserts with white cheese.

guayo grater. Used to shred root vegetables.

guineo banana.

guineo maduro ripe yellow banana. Eaten as a fruit.

guineo manzano apple banana. Eaten green as a **vianda** (root vegetable), or ripe, as a fruit.

guineo niño lady-finger banana. Eaten only when ripe. Dipped in flour and deep-fried, it is served as a side dish.

guineo verde green banana. Eaten as a side-dish starch. Green bananas are a part of the **viandas** family. The leaves are used to wrap **guanimes, pasteles,** and arroz apastelado.

guingambó okra.

guisado stewed.

haba lima bean.

habichuela bean. (See "The Basics," page 9.)

habichuela blanca white bean.

habichuela colorada small red kidney bean.

habichuela marca diablo red kidney bean.

habichuela rosada or **rosita** pink bean.

hoja de guineo banana leaf. Used to wrap **pasteles** and **guanimes**.

hojaldre puff pastry.

horchata de ajonjolí a drink made of ground sesame seeds, water, and sugar.

horno de microonda microwave oven.

jamón de cocinar smoked cooking ham. (See "The Basics," page 10.)

jíbaro envuelto lady-finger banana dipped in flour, fried, and served as a side dish.

juey Caribbean land crab.

langosta lobster. The lobster commonly found in the Caribbean Sea is the spiny or rock lobster. It is very hard to find on the mainland, but American (Maine) lobster can be substituted.

leche de coco coconut milk. (See "The Basics," page 9.)

lechón pig.

lechón asado a la varita a whole pig seasoned with **adobo** and cooked slowly over a charcoal pit.

lechón de mechar beef round cut, used on the island to make pot roast.

lechonera a stand where pit-roasted pig is sold by the pound or by the portion.

lechosa papaya. (See "The Basics," page 10.)

lerén a plant similar to a water chestnut, cultivated by the Taínos.

limber fruit juice frozen into ice cubes and eaten as a snack. The most famous **limbers** are sold in Old San Juan.

limón lemon.

limón verde a lime with very acidic juice, known on the mainland as key lime.

lima lime.

longaniza Spanish pork sausage, seasoned with **cilantro**, spices, and bay leaves. Used to make yellow rice.

mabí a fermented drink made from the bark of the **mabí** tree. On the island this is a daily drink. On the mainland, especially in the New York area, it is available only from April to September.

maicena cornstarch. Cornstarch is prepared as a hot breakfast cereal on the island, with milk and egg yolks. It is also used in the preparation of many custard desserts.

majarete a rice-flour dessert made during the Christmas season, especially on Three Kings Day (Epiphany).

malanga a root vegetable with brown skin and white or purple flesh. It is used to make **sancocho** and tripe soup. It is also boiled and served with salt codfish salad.

mamey a fruit with a rough brown skin and bright red flesh. It is mostly eaten in preserves and compotes. Fresh **mamey** is very hard to find, but the frozen pulp is available year-round in Hispanic markets.

mandarina mandarin orange.

mero red grouper. This fish is traditionally used to prepare **escabeche** during the Lent season.

mofongo fried green plantain mashed in a mortar and shaped into a ball. Traditionally it was seasoned with fresh garlic and pork cracklings. New versions are stuffed with seafood, chicken, or vegetables.

mojo a classic sauce that originated in the coastal town of Salinas, made with olives, tomato sauce, and vinegar.

mojo de ajo a garlic dipping sauce served with **tostones** or boiled cassava.

molleja chicken gizzard stewed in tomato sauce; usually served as an appetizer.

mondongo a thick soup made with beef tripe, assorted root vegetables, and seasonings.

morcilla blood sausage. A black sausage made from fresh pork blood and cooked rice. This is a traditional Christmas food.

naranja orange.

naranja agría sour orange, used mainly to prepare marinades. The white shell of the fruit is cooked in sugar and served as a dessert.

nuez moscada nutmeg.

ñame yam. A root vegetable with brown skin and white flesh. It is used in **sancocho** and eaten boiled.

olla soup pot. Usually made of aluminum.

oregano brujo Puerto Rican wild oregano. This oregano, with its distinctive pungent aroma, grows wild on the island. It is mostly used to make **sofrito**. It is very hard to find on the mainland.

paella a Spanish dish that consists of rice, saffron, **chorizo** and meat or seafood.

paellera a round, shallow iron pot with two handles, used to cook **paella**.

pana or **panapén** breadfruit. A round fruit with green skin and white flesh that came to the island from Tahiti. When green, it is eaten as a **vianda** or made into chips and **tostones**. When ripe, it is made into a dessert custard or boiled and mashed like potatoes. Breadfruit is available only during August and September. It can be stored in the refrigerator for a day or two and can also be frozen. Peel and remove the middle seed before cooking.

pana de pepita   breadfruit nut. A chestnutlike seed that is generally eaten boiled.

papa   potato.

parcha   passion fruit. (See "The Basics," page 10.)

pasteles   dumplings made from shredded root vegetables, stuffed with **picadillo** and boiled in banana or plantain leaves.

pasta de guayaba   guava paste. This is found in most *bodegas* and many supermarkets. It is used in many desserts, and as a jam.

pastel de masa   grated assorted root vegetables stuffed with pork, olives, and raisins and wrapped in banana leaves. A traditional Christmas food.

pastelón de plátano   yellow plantain pie made of fried slices of yellow plantain, beef **picadillo**, and green beans.

patas de cerdo   pig's feet. Usually prepared as a stew with chick-peas.

pegao   the crusty bottom of the rice that sticks to the pot. It is scraped and served with bean stew.

pernil de cerdo   pork shoulder.

picadillo   a basic beef stuffing mix made of ground beef, **sofrito**, raisins, and olives.

pique   vinegar seasoned with hot peppers, spices, and sour orange. Mostly used as a condiment.

pilón   mortar and pestle. A cooking utensil traditionally used to prepare **recaíto**. Taíno **pilónes** were made of stone. More recently they were made of wood; nowadays they are usually made of aluminum or plastic.

pimiento   bell pepper.

pimiento de cocinar   Italian frying pepper. (See "The Basics," page 11.)

pimiento morrón   roasted red pepper. Usually sold in cans or jars, preserved in water and salt. This is a classic garnish for rice dishes like **arroz con pollo**, potato salad, and **asopaos**.

pincho   skewered beef cubes.

piña   pineapple. The best pineapples grown on the island are from the Lajas Valley on the southwest coast. Puerto Rican pineapples are rarely available on the mainland, but the Hawaian pineapples available there can be used instead.

pinón de amarillo   yellow plantain pie.

piónono   a fritter made with yellow plantain. The plantain is cut lengthwise and fried. It is then shaped into a cup, stuffed with beef, chicken, or crab, sealed with eggs, and pan-fried.

plátano   plantain. (See "The Basics," page 11.)

plátano maduro   yellow plantain. (See "The Basics," page 11.)

plátano verde   green plantain. (See "The Basics," page 11.)

platanutre   plantain chip.

polvo de galleta   soda-cracker meal.

pote   an empty metal can, used in the old days as a cup to drink black coffee.

presa de pollo   chicken pieces.

punto de nieve   egg whites beaten until very stiff (literally, "snow peak").

quenepa   the fruit of a Caribbean tree, with green skin, pink flesh, and a large pit. The best ones are grown in Ponce, a town on the south coast of Puerto Rico. **Quenepas** are available fresh mostly during August. They are sold in bunches or packed in small plastic bags, and can be stored at room temperature.

queso blanco, queso de hoja or **queso del país**   Puerto Rican white cheese. A lightly salted white cheese made of cow's milk.

A distinctive characteristic of this cheese is that it does not melt.

queso de papa Cheddar cheese.

quimbombó okra.

recaíto a key seasoning in Puerto Rican cooking. It is a combination of onions, garlic, peppers, and **recao** or **cilantro.** (See "The Basics," page 11.)

recao green spiny leaf. (See "The Basics," page 11.)

relleno a fritter made of mashed potatoes stuffed with **picadillo,** shaped into a ball, and deep-fried. Canned corn beef is also used as a filling.

repollo cabbage.

salchicha Vienna sausage. (See "The Basics," page 11.)

salchichón salami. The salami used in Puerto Rico is similar to Genoa salami. **Salchichón** is widely available in *bodegas* and supermarkets.

salmorejo de jueyes crabmeat stew.

salsa de tomate tomato sauce. (See "The Basics," page 11.)

sancocho a thick soup made of assorted meats, root vegetables, **sofrito,** and corn on the cob, and traditionally served with plain white rice.

sangría Spanish wine punch.

sartén frying pan.

serenata de bacalao salt codfish salad. Made with salt codfish, potatoes, eggs, tomato, and avocado.

sirop syrup.

sofrito **recaíto** cooked with ham, **alcaparrado,** and tomato sauce. **Sofrito** is the base for many stews and sauces. (See "The Basics," page 11.)

sopón another name for **asopao**.

sorullo de maíz or **sorullito** a fritter made of cornmeal and shaped like a cigar, stuffed with cheese, and deep-fried. The most famous ones are made in Lajas, on Phosphorescent Bay (the same town where the island's best pineapples are grown). They are served with a sauce made of mayonnaise and ketchup.

sorbete sorbet.

tamarindo tamarind. (See "The Basics," page 12.)

tasajo Puerto Rican dry cured beef.

tayote another name for **chayote**.

tembleque a stirred custard made of coconut milk and sugar (literally "shaky").

tocino fatback. (See "The Basics," page 12.)

tomate tomato.

toronja grapefruit.

tostón a slice of green plantain fried, smashed flat, and refried.

tostonera the utensil traditionally used to prepare **tostones**. It is made of two flat pieces of wood screwed together. **Tostoneras** can be found in *bodegas* and supermarkets. If they are not available, smash the plantain between two pieces of plastic wrap or parchment paper.

turrón almond nougat. A sweet eaten during the Christmas season.

uva de playa sea grape.

verduras root vegetables.

viandas root vegetables. (See "The Basics," page 12.)

vinagre de manzana cider vinegar. (See "The Basics," page 12.)

yautía   taro root. (See "The Basics," page 12)

yuca   cassava, a root vegetable with hard white flesh and a rough brown skin. (See "The Basics," page 12.)

Mail Order Sources

Canada

Toronto Caribbean Corner
57 Kensington Avenue
Toronto, Ontario
(416) 593-0008
Caribbean foods

Tropical Harvest Food Market
57 Kensington Avenue
Toronto, Ontario
(416) 593-9279

North Central

La Preferida, Inc.
3400 West 35th Street
Chicago, IL 60632
(312) 254-7200

Middle Atlantic

Balducci's
424 Avenue of the Americas
New York, NY 10011
(212) 673-2600
Beans, cilantro, tropical fruits

Casa Hispanica International Food Market
P.O. Box 587
73 Poningo Street
Port Chester, NY 10578
(914) 939-9333
Caribbean foods

Dean and Deluca
560 Broadway
New York, NY 10012
(800) 221-7714
Boutique and regular beans, cilantro, annatto seeds, tropical fruits

Latin American Products
142 West 46th Street
New York, NY 10036
(212) 302-4323
Beans, Caribbean foods

Mountain

Earthstar Herb Gardens
P.O. Box 1022
Chino Valley, AZ 86323
(602) 636-4910
Fresh herbs

Pacific

Bean Bag
818 Jefferson Street
Oakland, CA 94607
1-800-845-BEANS

Caribbean Delites
1057 East Artesia Boulevard
Long Beach, CA 90805
(213) 427-5594
Caribbean foods

La Preferida, Inc.
4615 Alameda Street
Los Angeles, CA 90056
(213) 232-4322

Paradise Farms
1101 Eugenia, Suite B
Carpinteria, CA 93013
(805) 684-9468
Fresh herbs

Rosado's International Foods
1711 Little Orchard, Suite B
San Jose, CA 95125
(408) 298-2326

South Atlantic

Continental Trading Co.
7826 Easter Avenue, N.W.
Suite 500
Washington, D.C.
(202) 829-5620
Caribbean foods

Dekalb World Farmers Market
3000 East Ponce de León
Decatur, GA 30034
(404) 377-6401
Caribbean foods

Jamaica Groceries and Spices
9628 S.W. 160th Street
Colonial Shopping Center
Miami, FL 33157
(305) 252-1197
Caribbean foods

J. R. Brooks and Son, Inc.
P.O. Drawer 9
18400 S.W. 256th Street
Homestead, FL 33090-0009
(800) 327-4833
Tropical fruits

La Preferida, Inc.
9108 N.W. 105th Way
Medley, FL 33178
(305) 883-8444
Caribbean foods

West North Central

Herb Gathering, Inc.
5742 Kenwood Avenue
Kansas, City, MO 64110
(816) 523-2653
Fresh herbs

West South Central

La Preferida, Inc.
4000 Telephone Road
Houston, TX 77087
(713) 643-7128
Caribbean foods

Index

Index

Index

Index

Index

Index

Index

Index

Index